Presented To

Cedar Mill Community Library

In memory

of

John Schetky

TRUE
TASTE

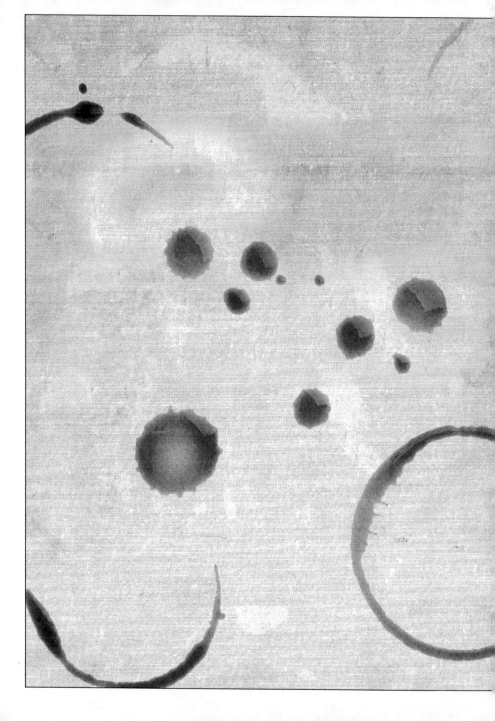

TRUE TASTE

The Seven Essential Wine Words

BY MATT KRAMER

CIDER MILL PRESS

BOOK PUBLISHERS

KENNEBUNKPORT, MAINE

13-Digit ISBN: 978-1604335682
10-Digit ISBN: 1604335688

This book may be ordered by mail from the publisher. Please include $4.95 for postage and handling. Please support your local bookseller first!

Books published by Cider Mill Press Book Publishers are available at special discounts for bulk purchases in the United States by corporations, institutions, and other organizations. For more information, please contact the publisher.

Cider Mill Press Book Publishers
"Where good books are ready for press"
12 Spring Street
PO Box 454
Kennebunkport, Maine 04046

Visit us on the Web! www.cidermillpress.com

Design by Jon Chaiet

1 2 3 4 5 6 7 8 9 0
First Edition

CONTENTS

ACKNOWLEDGMENTS

Nothing is more personal to an author than the Acknowledgments page. Although it seems to be a nation of one, a book is a country with an uncounted population not just of editors and publishers, but also of people who have supported an author in ways that provide him or her much-needed sustenance.

Foremost among them, at least in the most practical fashion, has been Marvin R. Shanken, the owner and editor of *Wine Spectator*. Without his support this book simply wouldn't have been possible. The opportunity to write regular, frequent columns for *Wine Spectator* has given me not just a financial endowment but also an intellectual one as well. I have had the privilege (that's the only word) of being allowed to think about wine week after week, year after year, and to articulate those thoughts to a sizable audience. This would not have been possible without Marvin Shanken's direct, personal support. To say that I am grateful understates the matter considerably.

Similarly, various editors over the years have weighed in with their thoughts, suggestions and revisions. Some of these I've grasped thankfully as if thrown a life preserver; others I've pushed away (foolishly, perhaps) and continued on my journalistic swim. Either way, I'm grateful for their always well-intentioned interest, support and practical help.

For this particular book I happily extend my sincere thanks to my longtime editor Carlo DeVito and to publisher John Whalen, whose love of wine and books is backed by their time, belief and, yes, checkbook. Thanks also are due to editor Diane Abrams for her careful reading of the manuscript and useful suggestions.

Not least, as always, is my wife, Karen. She has seen thousands of columns emerge, as well as an armload of books and has always assured me that the latest is the greatest. Of course, that's not always so. But it sure is nice to hear. I am endlessly grateful to her. Wherever I am and whatever I'm doing, she is always powerfully present.

PREFACE

I dream of lost vocabularies that might express some of what we no longer can.

— Jack Gilbert
The Great Fires: Poems 1982–1992

This is a book about judgment. I emphasize this point because to talk about wine today is to assume an analytical, almost forensic stance, which is pervasively seen in the now-ubiquitous "tasting note": a string of flavor descriptors punctuated by a point score. The only element of actual judgment too often is only the score itself.

Tasting-note flavor descriptors have become so elaborate—*maraschino cherry, graphite, road dust*—as to beg credulity and invite derision. Sure, it can be seen as simply comical. But apart from that and perhaps a certain amount of pretension, what's the harm? Little really, except for one not-so-small element that has changed the landscape of wine appreciation: The universal use of flavor descriptors, not just in wine writing but in wine education as well, powerfully suggests that taste acuity, i.e., the ability to distinguish an ever-longer list of scents, odors, aromas and flavors, is tantamount to judging the quality of a wine. It is nothing of the sort.

How and why flavor descriptors have become the prevailing—and limiting—vocabulary of wine appreciation merits its own discussion. (See page 13, "The Myths of Modern Wine Tasting.")

The language of wine has always been a central feature of wine appreciation. Language shapes thought.[1] How we talk about wine informs and colors not just our appreciation of it, but reveals which particular attributes persuade us to conclude that one wine is better than another.

True Taste: The Seven Essential Wine Words is not, of course, about a mere seven words. Instead, it's about those values that involve actual judgment, about the markers that help us navigate toward recognizing and understanding what makes one wine better than another, as well as assessing those writers or tasters who purport to do it for us.

In a democratic and populist culture, the idea that anything as subjective as wine—or any other sensory pleasure—can be declared "better" rubs against the grain. "If I like it, it's good" is the popular mantra. This is tasting as reactive emotion. It's a low bar, a minimal threshold. The fact is—and it *is* a fact—that good and less good exist independently of our personal preferences. There are scientific reasons involving human physiology and neurology that explain this more fully. More about that later in the book.

True Taste is about tasting wine with discernment rather than a game of I Spy flavor description. What may strike you as odd is that it's not about how to taste wine per se. This is because—this might surprise you— wine tasting really isn't very difficult. Almost anyone who's willing to pay attention and has just a modicum of experience can identify a better-quality wine from a lesser one. Really, it's no big deal.

Instead, the real challenge is putting words to wine. This is where many people—most, even—stumble. The vocabulary of wine is what's really daunting. The purpose of this book is to offer what the author believes is a more rewarding, more refreshing way to talk about wine through words that both identify and express the beauty we find in the glass.

"The universal use of flavor descriptors powerfully suggests that taste acuity is tantamount to judging the quality of a wine. It is nothing of the sort."

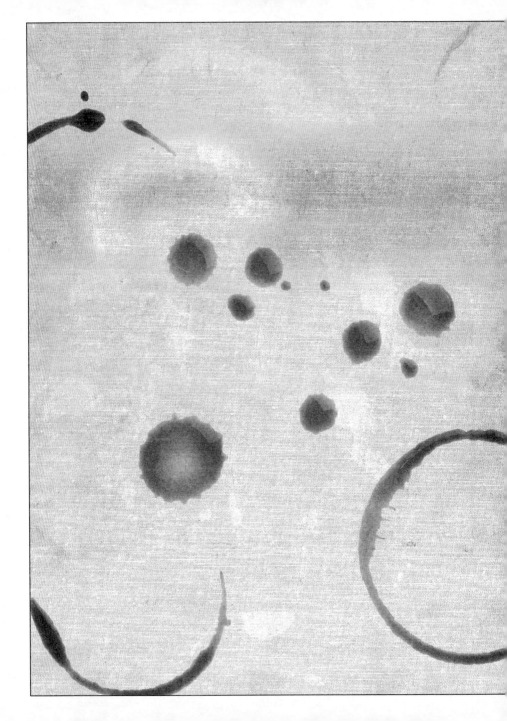

CHAPTER 1

THE MYTHS OF MODERN WINE TASTING

I should regard the critic as one of those beggars who sift the sand out of rivers to seek a few grains of gold.

—Denis Diderot
Écrits sur l'Art et l'Artiste

Wine tasting has evolved in recent years into something never previously seen in all the millennia that wines of quality have been drunk and discussed, which means at least as far back as the ancient Romans. (Pliny the Elder, writing in his *Natural History* about 1 A.D. goes into considerable, even geeky, detail about the fine wines of his time.)

Our moment is different. And you can date the origins of the change not to wine lovers, but to university professors—especially, but not exclusively, in the United States—in the field of wine science or enology.

Scientists of all sorts like to present themselves as disinterested observers. But their reality, like everyone else's, is that they necessarily must hustle and jostle in a professional and (academic) political context. It was no different in the academic discipline of enology, especially starting in the 1950s.

What happened can be expressed in two words: food processing. Of course, food processing has been going on for centuries. But it was only in the second half of the 20th century that food processing scaled-up to a deeply penetrating, mass market level. What was once localized to small companies that served their cities or regions became the province of national, and then international, corporations that researched, developed and released processed food products in vast quantities.

Of course, to achieve that sort of scale, as well as a

vital reliability and consistency, requires the sort of iron-grip control that scientific methods alone can achieve. "Artisanal" is not a term of admiration in such an environment.

Now, while food scientists at agricultural colleges across the nation were engaged in increasingly respected—and lucrative, in terms of research funding—scientific experiments in service to the ever-larger food processors, their colleagues in the emergent field of wine science had no such respect and even fewer monetary opportunities.

The reason, of course, was that wine in the United States was still embryonic after the devastation of Prohibition, which lasted from 1920 to 1933. The wine science professors at the University of California, Davis wanted to take their rightful place among their professional colleagues as scientists of equal standing and esteem.

At the same time, what was needed—and able to be funded—in California wine was the mass market needs of bulk wine producers, epitomized by Gallo. Indeed, more than any of the other bulk wine producers at the time (and there were many more in the 1950s and '60s than exist today), Gallo was singularly aware of the uses of wine science in creating a consistent and regularized product from something that was previously perceived as inherently subjective and resistant to controlled uniformity.

From this emerged a powerful push on the part of wine science professors everywhere in the world, but especially in California, to create not only a rigorous scientific methodology for tasting wines, but also a transformed vocabulary of wine appreciation.

Words such as *nuance, finesse, subtle, elegant,* and dozens of other long-used wine appreciation terms were dismissed as vague and inherently subjective. They sought instead to cultivate a vocabulary that was scientific—and repeatable in controlled settings—in its precision. The language of traditional wine connoisseurship was scorned as poetic and fanciful.

So-called scientific wine tasting is designed for statistically verifiable repetition meant for the needs of large-scale producers who seek a rigorous uniformity of taste consistency. If the wine scientists could have created such a thing, they would gladly have replaced inherently unreliable human tasters with machines that can taste for specific features with unerring consistency and accuracy. (That day is very nearly here, by the way.)[2]

Since they couldn't do that, the next best thing was to somehow make human tasters as machine-like as possible. That meant emphasizing only those elements that could be repeatedly identified by human tasters to a satisfactory degree of statistical reliability.

This desire was never better captured than in *Wines:*

Their Sensory Evaluation (1976) by Maynard A. Amerine and Edward B. Roessler, two UC Davis professors who intended the book, quite amazingly, for a popular readership. It's amazing because nearly half of the book's 204 pages are devoted to statistical procedures. Although never a best-seller, this book was influential and epitomized the perspective of wine scientists on the subject of sensory evaluation. Professor Amerine (1911–1998) was unquestionably America's most influential wine scientist; Professor Roessler (1902–1993) was a prominent mathematician at UC Davis.

"Our basic premise," they wrote, "is that wine consumers and professional enologists alike will enjoy their wines more and will make more intelligent decisions about wine quality and wine value if they understand how and why they make such decisions and how to determine, when necessary, the statistical significance of those decisions."

It's a myth that "scientific" wine tasting has any validity in the real life of wine drinkers. In fairness to wine scientists and their methodology, it never was intended to. The ability to repeatedly nail the taste or scent of, say, almonds, in a "blind" taste test is critical only to tasters involved in product development or quality testing. But what do such skills have to do with judgment? Nothing, really. It's like asking a sharpshooter to evaluate battlefield strategy.

All the wine scientists were (and are) trying to achieve in their tasting methodology is a statistically valid replicability of results. Does a panel of tasters trained to recognize specific features in a wine, especially defects such as volatile acidity or brettanomyces, consistently do so in blind taste tests? If they do (and, yes, they can) then the tasting is deemed "scientific."

Just why wine tasting is supposed to achieve "scientific" results is itself a curiosity. No other aesthetic achievement has such a demand placed upon it. Can you imagine a ballet performance being "scientifically" assessed? Or a chamber music concert being judged solely on the basis of intonation and note-for-note perfection? ("The concert was great. Everyone was in tune and no wrong notes were heard.")

That's the back story, as they say in Hollywood. What happened next changed everything. The wine academics had their say and sway with several generations of scientifically-trained winemakers. But the influence of the academy really didn't reach consumers. Wine writers, however, did. And unlike anything previously seen in the once-staid world of (mostly British) wine writing, the new American wine critics changed the landscape.

Starting in the 1970s, the first thing these new, young American wine critics did was review a lot more wines than their predecessors. Where once tasting 30 wines of a given type (red Bordeaux, Chianti, white Burgundy) was seen as a thoroughly professional job, the new critics thought nothing of reviewing 200 such wines. After all, the last 40 years have seen a gusher of new producers from Europe, the Americas, and Australia and New Zealand.

That, in turn, created a practical problem: How do you impose order on such abundance? Where before, with a modest number of wines, it was practical enough to (unequally) divide 30 or so wines into categories such as fair, good or exceptional, with 200 or more wines such broad divisions bloat into ineffectiveness. The eye glazes over. This is why the 100-point scoring system emerged and was embraced by readers.

Whatever its deficiencies—and there are many—the 100-point system brings order to chaos. Scores are instantly intuitive. That's why they are potent. A wine with 91 points is, obviously, considered superior to one awarded 89 points. (Of course, how a critic arrives at such a precise difference of a mere two points is another matter altogether.)

This modern abundance of wines and the Faustian desire on the part of some wine publications to evaluate seemingly all wines from everywhere has brought us to the now-ubiquitous tasting note.

You, the reader, want to know what a wine tastes like. It's not enough (it never was) for a reviewer to say, "This here red Burgundy is really good." Never mind that. What does it *taste* like?

Here, the wine scientists surfaced. Their sensory evaluation terminology, designed for controlled environment taste testing, emphasized flavor descriptors. Ann C. Noble, a chemist with a doctorate in food science who was a longtime professor at UC Davis, invented what she called the Wine Aroma Wheel. This pie-shape diagram divides broad categories, such as *fruity*, into subsets, such as *citrus, berry* and *tropical fruit*, which are then further subdivided in their respective categories into *grapefruit, blackberry, banana*, and so forth.

The Aroma Wheel made broadly popular what wine scientists had been promulgating for decades, namely an absolute and unwavering rejection of all subjective or "hedonic" terminology in favor of specific, replicable, repeatable terms that are "useful" (her word) in wine evaluation.

At the professional level, with thousands of wines a year to review, writers had no choice. How many times can you describe a Pinot Noir as being *cherry-scented*? So you get more specific, summoning up *black cherry, wild cherry, pie cherry, maraschino cherry, cherry jam* and *cherry liqueur.*

From there, descriptors ramped-up to become ever more inventive and specific, embracing the likes of *honeysuckle, heather, coffee*, every imaginable sort of tea, *bergamot* (think Earl Grey), various sorts of peaches,

"The Holy Grail of objectivity is hoisted whenever someone disputes another's conclusion about a wine. It's 'subjective,' they say, which invalidates whatever is submitted (and serves to reaffirm the unassailability of one's own conclusion)."

all kinds of chocolates, baked desserts, various wood scents, and a quarry-full of rocks such as *slate, chalk, road dust, gravel, the-scent-of-gravel-after-a-summer-rain*, as well as *graphite, tar* and so forth.

I am sympathetic to my wine-tasting colleagues. Readers do want to know what a wine tastes like. After 200 or 400 wines, what are you going to say? "I really like this wine" simply won't satisfy.

Flavor descriptors in themselves aren't the problem. The problem is that the near-exclusive use of them in "discussing" wine leaves wine drinkers with the impression that, if you can't find all these flavors, you as a taster of wine are somehow lacking. This was perfectly captured by one of my readers who commented about "those among us who enjoy wine but might not have the keen enough sense of smell and taste to identify notes of *decaying burlap hanging from a Japanese maple.*"

Here we arrive at the critical—in every sense—matter of judgment. Flavor descriptors have nothing to do with judgment. What you can find doesn't necessarily correspond to what you conclude.

The number or variety of descriptors that can be identified says little about the quality of the wine. At most, identifying an array of flavors and scents might tell us something about a wine's complexity. But that still doesn't address how well those flavors cohere. More than a few such "complex" wines quickly fatigue the drinker. What initially seems kaleidoscopic and exciting can sometimes, although not always, become irritating. An abundance of flavor descriptors in a tasting note tells us surprisingly little about a wine's actual quality.

Unfortunately, too many tasting notes now offer little more than a string of fanciful flavor descriptors with the judgment revealed only in the score itself—a numerical "thank you ma'am" after the much more energetic "slam, bam" of the flavor descriptors.

As the preceding discussion explains, the source of insisting upon the plausibility and desirability of scientific wine tasting can be directly traced to the professional interests of wine scientists seeking academic respectability among their peers as well as serving the narrow needs of wine processing.

This in turn has created the other great myth of modern wine tasting: the notion of objectivity. The Holy Grail of objectivity is hoisted whenever someone disputes another's conclusion about a wine. It's "subjective," they say, which invalidates whatever is submitted (and serves to reaffirm the unassailability of one's own conclusion).

"Objectivity" in wine tasting does exist. But it exists on such a small plane, in such a confined fashion (such as a blind "triangle tasting") as to render it more a laboratory reality than a real-life one, like one of those

"One of the myths of modern wine tasting is the conviction that we are so flawed, so biased, that we are inherently unreliable as judges unless a wine is evaluated 'blind.' This is the Original Sin school of wine tasting."

elements in the periodic table that exist only for mere fractions of a second in a particle accelerator.

For wine objectivists blind tasting is always the best way to judge wine. I emphasize *always* because it's the key word. Blind tasting, where you can't see the label, is a useful way to taste wine and an excellent teaching tool. But it is by no means always the ideal.

It's necessary to distinguish between different types of blind tasting. You can have what's called a "single-blind" tasting, where you know one or more of several features of the wines under consideration, such as grape variety, vintage, country or region or district of origin, and so forth.

Then there's what's called a "double-blind" tasting where you don't know anything at all about the wine: color, name, origin, price, grape variety or producer. (In academic settings "double-blind" has a different meaning: not only don't you know what's being served, but neither does the server. This removes any unconscious clues we might signal as a server or somehow pick up as a taster.)

Then there's the academic gold standard of blind tasting, the narrow and sharply focused "triangle test." The Society of Sensory Professionals (an academic association) describes a triangle test this way:

"A panelist is presented with one different and two alike samples. If possible, all three samples should be presented to the panelist at once, and the panelist should be instructed to taste the samples from left to right. The six possible order combinations should be randomized across panelists."

How is a triangle test used? The Society of Sensory Professionals explains, quite clearly, the utility of this sort of blind tasting:

"For example, a baking company recently reformulated their famous peanut butter cookie in order to reduce costs. The company wished to know if the reformulation was identical to the original. The researchers administered a triangle test to a panel of 60 tasters. The panel obtained 24 correct answers."[3]

But what has blind tasting, never mind the methodology, to do with judging the quality of a wine? At a basic level, blind tasting is useful for general assessment and, especially, for isolating defects. But its greatest appeal is that blind tasting is ideal for eliminating bias and prejudice.

This last point makes blind tasting seem, to a popular audience, the "fairest" way to taste wine. The populist appeal of blind tasting lies in its reflection of Lord Chief Justice Gordon Hewitt's famous dictum, "Not only must Justice be done; it must also be *seen to be done.*" (Emphasis his.)

A vast body of evidence demonstrates that we are all susceptible to bias or prejudice in evaluating wines (and many other things). If a wine has a famous name or a high price we tend to deem it superior. This is a fact, and there's no disputing it.

However, one of the myths of modern wine tasting is the conviction that we are so flawed, so biased, that we are inherently unreliable as judges unless a wine is evaluated "blind." This is the Original Sin school of wine tasting. We are weak creatures and so filled with bias as to preclude "objectivity." Therefore, any judgment made about a wine is seen as suspect, if not invalid, unless tasted blind.

This is a simplistic, schoolboy notion of "fairness." It is popularly persuasive because of its Manichean worldview: the sanitizing light of unbiased, "objective" blind tasting against the murky, suspicious twilight of wines tasted with the labels on view.

This devout belief in blind tasting conveniently side-steps (because it can't be scientifically proved) that we can, if we wish, adjust or compensate for our biases. For example, there's no question that if I know that I'm tasting La Tâche, a famous red Burgundy that costs several thousand dollars a bottle, I am certainly inclined to find virtues in it and to discount any deficiencies.

But knowing that it's La Tâche also makes a positive difference involving "fairness" as well. I know, as do many other tasters, that La Tâche is a wine that can take 10 or 20 years to reveal all its virtues. A just-released latest vintage is often not all that impressive.

So just how "fair" is it to toss that latest-vintage La Tâche into a blind tasting with a bunch of other Pinot Noirs, some of which might shine luminously in their extreme youth, and then declare: "We tasted it fair and square with everything blind and the La Tâche came in dead last." (Believe me, this sort of thing happens all the time.)

What often goes unmentioned is how easily you can arrange a blind tasting in such a fashion as to virtually guarantee that a certain sort of wine will always triumph or fail to impress. Our biases go way beyond the prurience of seeing a glimpse of seductive label peeking out.

In a blind tasting, where everyone is groping in the darkness, the structural truth is that while experienced tasters will indeed select better over lesser wines, once that first cut is made they will then gravitate to those (good) wines that offer bigger, more accessible fruit and depreciate the more austere, less showy versions. This occurs not just regularly but almost invariably, especially in large-scale blind tastings. The more wines being tasted at one time, the more likely that bigger, showier, more accessible wines will be deemed best in a blind tasting.

That noted, blind tasting absolutely has legitimate uses. It serves admirably, even vitally, as a means to create a level playing field for new or unknown or unheralded wines that want or deserve to "get into the club." When, for example, in the 1970s and '80s California wine producers wanted to demonstrate to doubters that their Cabernets were the equal to the best in the world, the most effective and persuasive way to do so was to put them into blind tastings against the most famous red Bordeaux. It took a lot of just such tastings to finally nullify the incredulity, but it worked. And it was an appropriate methodology, too.

But the advantages of blind tasting rapidly diminish once the hurdle of incredulity or ignorance (whether prejudiced or otherwise) has been surmounted. Fine wines, like people, can only be properly assessed one at a time, in all sorts of settings. Only then does a "content of character" make itself known. And that requires not just repeated exposure over many vintages, but knowledge about precisely what it is that you're tasting, the better to evaluate the wine for what you know it should be, rather than trying to figure out what it might be.

Wine tasting today must contend with several pressures simultaneously. One is the inappropriate intrusion of scientific parameters upon fundamentally aesthetic matters. Another is simply handling the flood of wines that need and deserve to be tasted. How you choose the "best" methodology and then describe your conclusions invites its own set of biases, influences, possibilities and pitfalls. But one thing is certain: The best way to taste is the one that lends itself to a judgment founded on the values that really matter.

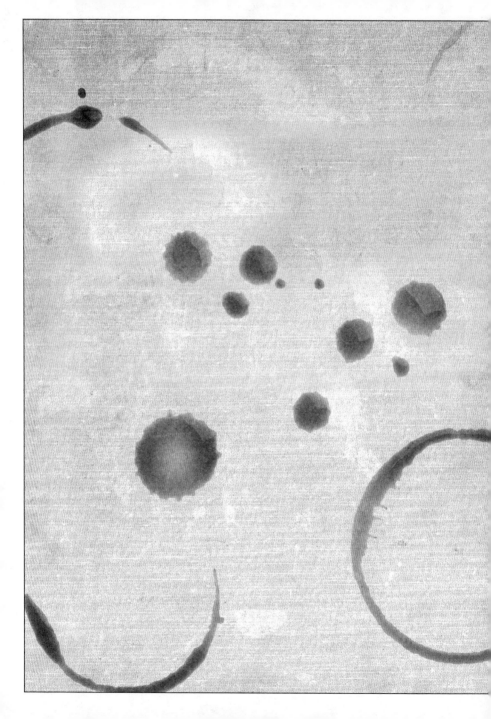

tradition of British wine writing as we know it today. The educations these gentlemen wine traders received at their public schools and universities gave them a respect for, and a liking of, scholarship. So they freely had at least a go at writing on the subject literally at hand, namely, wine.

Inevitably, much of it was drivel along the lines of, "We had a jolly good time visiting old so-and-so in his cellar in Reims, etc." But a substantial amount of serious and thoughtful wine scholarship also emerged, often penned by men (there were no women in the British wine trade until quite recently) who had decades of experience tasting and discussing a very narrow range of wines limited mostly to red Bordeaux (aka claret), Champagne, Sherry, Burgundy, Port and German wines (aka hock). Other wines were seen and tasted, but only rarely were they subjected to any sort of investigatory scholarship. Narrow it may have been, but they knew what they were talking about. They were connoisseurs.

Above all, they gave their clients not just a taste for wine, but also for wine advice. Through their writings they made it clear how much the appreciation of fine wine required and rewarded a bit of instruction. This alone separated British wine lovers from their Continental brethren, who felt no need for such self-improvement. Of course, it also served to make these same merchants indispensable. Without them one was

CHAPTER 2

INSIGHT

Experience + Thought + Synthesis = Insight

So much about wine involves evaluation. Not only does fine wine invite analysis and discussion, it virtually demands it. Can anything more damning be said about a wine than, "There's not much to say about it"?

What is less often addressed is, for lack of a better phrase, evaluating the evaluation. Put another way: We're given an awful lot of advice these days. How does one weigh its worth?

Once, the advisory offerings were few. You had a handful of so-called "wise men" who either worked in the wine trade and proffered advice to their customers or a handful of wine critics who, by dint of publishing extensive tasting notes, presented themselves as authorities worth following. Both groups had—and still have—their virtues.

Traditionally, wine writing was the province of the British wine trade. It was the British who invented wine writing as we know it today. Onlookers to wine might understandably assume that the French or Italians have a long tradition of writing for an eager wine-interested public, but it's not so. There's surprisingly little history of wine writing in either France or Italy even though both nations flood the world with wines.

Very likely it's the sheer abundance of native wine that makes the French and Italians disinterested in advice; every French person or Italian I've met seems quite certain of his or her own tastes in matters of wine. And besides, what's all the fuss? Wine is seen as an everyday commodity, like bread and salt. What's to investigate? Exceptions to this blithe self-assurance exist, but they are surprisingly rare in France and Italy to this day. The old saying got it wrong: Familiarity (with wine) actually breeds content. The contempt is for presumptuous wine critics who would disturb it.

Just why the British evolved into a different wine culture is not difficult to parse. Although wine grapes have always been grown in England particularly (and there's more today than has been seen for at least a century), Britain is not a significant wine producer. Wine is an imported item and consequently a mercantile matter.

Add to that the "gentlemen's trade" aspect to traditional British wine mercantilism. If, upon graduating from Oxford or Cambridge, you didn't go into the military, the Church or the City (i.e., finance), then a gentleman could pursue wine as one of the few socially acceptable forms of trade (a word then said with an ill-concealed curl of the lip). Wine at least had a certain cachet, even if one was reduced to selling it. In the old days those sales were themselves confined—at least for fine wines—to a select circle, which was why it was a gentleman's calling.

It's too easy to caricature all this (and no one has done so better than the British themselves), but the fact remains that one benefit was, if nothing else, the

lost in the bewilderment of fine wine—or so you were led to believe.

This genteel tradition crossed the Atlantic and took root in New York, Boston and Philadelphia, extending even to San Francisco. But well into the mid-20th-century it was, as in Great Britain, confined to a relatively small circle of sellers and buyers. Fine wine, on both sides of the Atlantic, was a clubby thing, literally and figuratively.

Then came democratization. This was inevitable as economic wealth increased and even exploded starting in the 1960s and later. Democratization of fine wine occurred not just at the public level, where a newly well-educated and aspirational middle class acquired a taste and the means for finer things, but also in the wine business itself.

Take, for example, how Bordeaux wines traditionally were bought and sold at the wholesale level. Until the 1960s, Bordeaux wines were purchased in barrel by a handful of wealthy négociants or shippers, most of them located on a single stretch of grand warehouses called the Quai des Chartrons in the city of Bordeaux. (Collectively these shippers were known as the Chartronnais.) By virtue of their wealth—necessary because until the 1960s Bordeaux wines typically were held in cask and bottle for as long as a decade before being sold—and connections to the growers, as well as owning prominent wine châteaux themselves, they ruled the worldwide Bordeaux trade with an absolutism that even Louis XIV would have envied.

Then democracy arrived, mostly in the form of American capitalism. Big liquor companies, notably Seagram but also Hueblein and National Distillers, as well as English brewing companies, such as Bass Charrington, were awash in profits from booze (which was then, and still is today, far more lucrative than wine) and beer. They saw that there was a nice buck to be made from Bordeaux wine thanks to a newly emerging affluent middle class.

The short version of what happened next was that the big booze and beer money both dwarfed and humbled the Bordeaux shippers, the once-feared "aristocracy of the cork." These new importers were rich enough to buy and store the wines themselves, thank you very much. So they bypassed the shippers and went directly to the growers, reducing the once-omnipotent shippers to being "sample carriers" earning a commission. It forever changed the way Bordeaux was bought and sold. (The shippers still exist, by the way, as they are a hardy, crafty lot. But their power has never since been the same.)

This new democratization eventually extended to the insular world of (then still mostly British) wine writing. Precisely because it was drawn exclusively from the wine trade, the line between wine discussion and commercial self-interest was no line at all. At best, it was blurred. At worst it was utterly duplicitous, with ostensibly disinterested—as far as the average reader knew—wine writers praising the very producers they were selling. Real scholarship was also offered, it must be said.

The American approach was fundamentally different, taking its cue not from the self-interest of the trade, but from the purposeful neutrality of outsider journalism. Recall that it was the era of Ralph Nader and, later, Watergate. American writers' perspective— and those of their publishers—were those of the consumer, although more than a little chumminess existed between the usually freelance wine writers and the wine trade that offered them tastings, trips and sometimes lavish lunches.

Most independent and rigorous of all were the handful of critics who were their own publishers, selling their wine evaluation newsletters to paying subscribers and taking no advertising. A.J. Liebling's famous dictum was their rallying cry: "Freedom of the press is guaranteed only to those who own one." These newsletter critics took on the task of tasting seemingly all wine from everywhere and taking not a penny in advertising. They changed the game, bringing both journalistic ethics and a certain fearlessness to the sometimes obscurantist and often compliant world of trade-driven wine writing.

Whether these newcomers were qualified for their task of wine evaluation was—and is—entirely a separate matter. The "wise men" of the Old School certainly had many vintages worth of experience behind their judgments, however opaquely expressed. ("A useful vintage" was a common euphemism for a lousy wine from a poor year that still, of course, had to be sold.)

If the comparative inexperience of the New School (mostly American) wine writers bothered its practitioners, they never let on. Soon enough they acquired a kind of experience in an intensive fashion thanks to massive tastings, much like taking an immersion course in a foreign language.

All of which brings us to the only thing that matters: Insight. All the experience in the world is of little use unless its primary objective is acquiring and transmitting insight. The only question a reader need ask when evaluating a wine writer is: How much insight is he or she seeking to provide?

This may seem a daunting or inappropriate demand on the part of someone who insists—rightly or not—that he or she knows little about wine. But it takes very little exposure to get a sense of whether someone is conveying not just information ("As of 2010 Burgundy has 41 *grands crus.*") but a more considered conclusion derived from a thoughtful sifting-through. More than ever before, this is the modern challenge of both writing wine criticism today and reading it.

It hardly needs saying that wine opinion is everywhere today. *Vox populi*—the voice of the people—has never been more amplified, for reasons that need no explanation. Seemingly everyone who's ever tasted a wine now has a public opinion on the subject. We are deluged with tasting notes plumped with flavor descriptors not just in print publications (which give a writer an aura of institutional authority, whether deserved or not), but on Internet wine cellar databases, personal blogs and wine chat boards where Jane and Joe Everyman can post his or her own tasting notes.

There's nothing wrong with this democratization of wine opinion and a very great deal that's right with it. But differentiating between mere opinion and actually saying something worthwhile calls for selectivity on the part of the recipient. Precisely because everyone now offers a tasting note and a score, it's essential to ask: What do they have to say? What is really on offer beyond a wine version of a gunslinger's scorekeeping notch in the handle?

This is why the next phase in our new wine democracy requires a filter for insight. It's no longer sufficient to say that you've tasted this wine or visited that vineyard. Never mind what the experience brought to you.

What did *you* bring to it? What did you extract, courtesy of your intellect and prior experience, that tells the rest of us something new or original? In short, what insight are you offering or at least seeking?

Now, insight isn't easy. And it's not always available or appropriate for all wine writing occasions. Sometimes, to borrow from Sigmund Freud, a tasting note is just a tasting note. But such notes alone do not suffice, as they typically tell us little or nothing about the worth or basis of the judgment rendered. Too often they exist in a vacuum.

Insight, as expressed in the formula in the title of this chapter, is the product of Experience + Thought + Synthesis. Each of these alone is insufficient; it's a classic "sum greater than its parts."

Experience alone is often thought to be all that's needed. This is understandable if only because experience comprises the building blocks of insight. It's impossible to arrive at anything resembling insight without a context, which is to say, experience. Without having tasted a lot of one type of wine or another, how can you possibly approach anything like an insightful observation? Obviously, you can't.

But experience alone is deceptive. First, not all wine experiences are of equal value. There is tasting and there is tasting, as it were. Visiting producers on site, walking through their vineyards with them and then

"It's not enough simply to taste a lot of wines. I've met many people who have tasted thousands of wines. And God knows, they have opinions. But too often they have little to say. Instead, they mostly offer reactions: it was good, it was bad. They imagine this to be thought. But it's more akin to data processing."

tasting their wines from both barrel and bottle with them is an entirely different tasting experience than— as is typical in modern wine sales—having the local distributor come by and (odd expression this) "tasting you" on their latest offerings. In both cases each can say that they tasted so-and-so's wines. But one tasting is profoundly more substantial than the other.

So right there alone, it helps to know how and when— in what fashion and under what circumstance—a wine was tasted. Some readers insist that only a blind tasting tells the truth. I am not of that opinion myself, for reasons previously detailed. But it's a useful piece of information to know, all the same.

The second element of the equation, Thought, is not quite as obvious as it may seem. Too many tasters merely react to a wine, typically landing on one side or the other of the I-like-it-or-I-don't divide. Too many tasters, never mind how experienced, do not tailor their criteria to the wine cloth at hand.

You can see this, for example, in tasters who specialize in assessing Cabernet Sauvignon and Bordeaux when they offer judgments about Pinot Noir. Where the latter wine is all about—or should be, anyway—nuance, finesse and subtlety, the Cabernet-oriented tasters apply criteria that often skew their preferences to Pinot Noirs that offer power, scale and forthrightness, like roughhousing a cat the way you would with a dog.

You would think that experience alone would preclude this sort of thing, but it doesn't. It takes thought. And care. And consideration. Every wine must be approached differently, and one has to be both thoughtful and careful in recognizing that criteria for insightful evaluation must necessarily be different.

This is why there is no such thing as a Universal Taster, never mind those wine writers who issue a vast array of tasting notes on seemingly all wines from everywhere. It's highly unlikely that an expert on Renaissance art is also equally at home with contemporary art. Each is understood using very different criteria and must be assessed accordingly. It's no different with wine.

Finally, we arrive at Synthesis. In some ways, this is the key. How many people have we met who have an array of talents, sometimes dazzlingly so, but they lack that one additional talent, namely, the one that would have helped him or her use all the others. That's synthesis. Call it connecting the dots if you like.

It's not enough simply to taste a lot of wines. I've met many people who have tasted thousands of wines. And God knows, they have opinions. But too often they have little to say. Instead, they mostly offer reactions: it was good, it was bad, it wasn't as good as this producer or that vintage. They imagine this to be thought. But it's more akin to data processing. An index, however useful, is not the book itself.

As the catalytic element of insight, synthesis is hardest to achieve if only because you can't force it. It arrives in its own good time, as you really can't compel yourself to correlate all you have experienced or even thought about. It seems to come of its own accord.

I experienced just such a moment while writing *Making Sense of Burgundy* (1990). I visited producer after producer, methodically going from one village in the Côte d'Or to the next. There's no little repetition in such visits, as they usually take the same form from one (small) grower to the next. You get into a pattern and repetition of questions, trying to tease out both factual information and quicksilver insights from farmers who, like farmers everywhere, are disinclined to articulate such things.

There are tricks you can use, by the way. I once wrote a newspaper column titled "How To Be A Wine Guy" where I described just such a trick, acquired during my Burgundy book experience.

"When the time comes for The Tasting," I wrote, "you project floods of modesty and self-effacement (this is hardest part for me). You say that, really, if the grower would be so kind, if he wouldn't mind, you would like to taste the wines blind and say where they came from."

"Six glasses are put in front of you on an upended barrel. ...You swirl. You sniff. And you spit with a certain definitiveness. (Really good spitting is something I've never mastered. This is a pity because people always credit a good spitter with having a great palate.) Eventually you hold forth. Here, you let slip your veil of modesty. You verbally stride forth, saying, 'I think this first wine is the Serpentières because it has that ethereal delicacy I always associate with this vineyard.'

"This, of course, is nonsense. You haven't a clue. But you persist, going down the line, declaring with professional certitude the distinctions of each wine that unmistakably make it such-and-such vineyard. By now, the winegrower can barely contain himself. He's practically hopping from one foot to the other like a schoolboy with an overfull bladder. He can't wait to gleefully tell you how wrong you are. And, boy, are you ever wrong. In all the years I've been pulling this stunt, not once have I ever been right."

Now, comes the hoped-for benefit of The Trick:

"The winegrower, with the sort of false dejection seen at the best funerals, declares that he's so sorry, *monsieur*, but the first wine is not Serpentières. 'No, *monsieur*, it is the Jarrons vineyard. You see, Jarrons has a rich, meaty quality due to the high clay content, etc.' While the grower is expansive with an eloquence and articulateness you couldn't get from him if you asked a direct question, you are scribbling like mad. Word for word, you download this distilled wisdom of generations of winegrowers."

Such shenanigans aside, I asked each grower what they thought was the single best vineyard in their village. Usually there was a consensus, such as Chambertin in Gevrey-Chambertin, Meursault "Perrières," Volnay "Caillerets" or Romanée-Conti in Vosne-Romanée.

I carefully noted this accrued information and filed it away in my head. But it was only after the book was published that a certain insight arrived. I realized that there was a common denominator to all of the vineyards that growers declared to be their single best. But I didn't see it in time for the book, which I still regret. As I said, you can't force this business of connecting the dots.

The common denominator was (and still is) that each of the vineyards cited as "best" represents a consolidation of attributes rather than an exemplar of one or another. In Gevrey-Chambertin, for example, there are seven *grands crus*, which is a remarkable number for one small village. Each of these *grands crus* has its signature quality. For example, Griotte-Chambertin is notable for an intense wild cherry scent and taste, hence *griotte* (wild cherry). Mazi-Chambertin is considered to be the most *sauvage* or wild-tasting; Ruchottes-Chambertin is thought the most stony-tasting.

Yet Chambertin was and still is collectively seen by the producers in Gevrey-Chambertin as their single best vineyard. Why? Because it consolidates more attributes in one wine than any of the others. It has some of the *sauvagerie* of Mazi along with some of the wild cherry of Griotte and some of the stoniness of Ruchottes, among other attributes. No other vineyard site, even among the *grands crus*, can do the same. It is first among equals.

The same conclusion, I realized, was true all along the line of the Côte d'Or. A collective aesthetic had emerged in Burgundy over centuries that prized this singular capacity to consolidate all or most of the attributes of the neighboring vineyards in a single site.

Seeking insight, no matter how slight, is what matters, never more so than now. It always mattered, of course. But today's abundance of "data points," all those discrete tasting notes, adds a certain urgency to this need for insight. Put another way, insight is the search engine algorithm that allows us to connect with what we really need to know about wine. It's what we, as tasters, should seek from ourselves and, as readers, should ask from others.

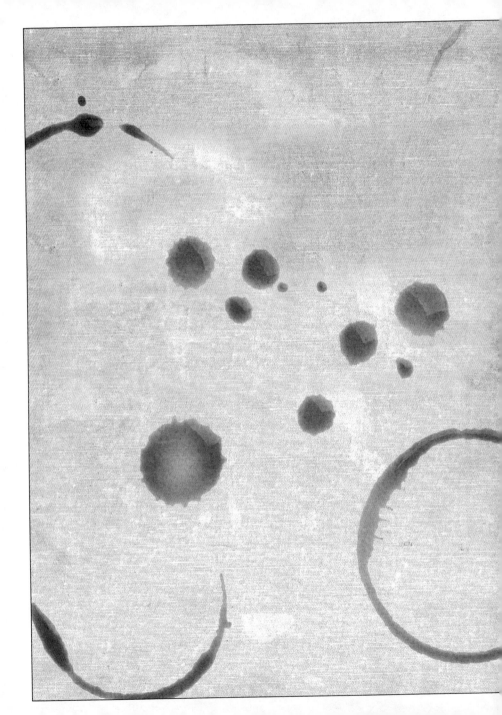

CHAPTER 3

HARMONY

A man shall see faces, that if you examine them part by part, you shall find never a good; and yet altogether do well.

—Francis Bacon
Essays, Civil and Moral

There is no correct or ideal way to view wine. But one useful approach is to see wine as a collection of forces. These include, but are not confined to, such elements as tannins, acidity, fruit, alcohol and sweetness.

There is yet another force that's worth mentioning, which is the unseen cohesion called harmony. By chance I learned about its essential quality in one of the earliest–and best–wine lessons of my life. I was interviewing Edmond Maudière, who, in the 1970s, was the *chef de cave* or head winemaker for Moët et Chandon, the big Champagne house.

In the early 1970s Moët had decided to create a California outpost and sent Maudière to Napa Valley to oversee the fledgling wine production of the new Domaine Chandon.

You might be amused to learn that, prior to his arrival, Domaine Chandon's small (and very young) staff at the time were terrified that Maudière—who, after all, occupied the highest winemaking position of the largest Champagne producer in the world—would be one of those relentlessly formal Frenchmen who insists upon wearing a jacket and tie. Such Frenchmen existed in abundance back then. But Edmond Maudière was nothing of the sort. From the first day, Maudière loved California's casual, freewheeling style and always wore blue jeans—except when his French bosses arrived from Champagne. (He later settled in California upon retirement and started a consulting service.)

Anyway, I went to Napa Valley to interview Edmond Maudière for a national food and wine magazine. I was at the beginning of my career and consequently knew only a sprinkle about wine and barely a drop, if that, about sparkling wine. Maudière was a wonderful teacher and taught me a lesson about harmony that I have never forgotten.

"When you create a sparkling wine you can never lose sight of the power and influence of the bubbles," he said. "Why? Because bubbles magnify. So when you create the blend—and as you know nearly all sparkling wines, especially in Champagne, are blends not only of several grape varieties but of many different vine-yards—you must always keep in mind the magnifying power of the bubbles.

"So when you create a blend for the base wine—before the secondary fermentation which creates the bubbles—you have to imagine what the blend will be like *after* being magnified by the bubbles. Any flaw in the blend, even a tiny one barely perceptible in the base wine, will be enlarged." It was at that point that he introduced his concept of the "perfect sphere."

"The ideal in blending is to create a perfect sphere," he said. "Think of it this way: A perfect sphere can descend to any depth of the ocean and never break because the pressure on all sides is equal at all times.

"To achieve this ideal 'perfect sphere' there must be as great a harmony in the blend as possible. This is why sparkling wine is such a great challenge. You must strive to create the harmony of a perfect sphere."

I have never forgotten this lesson. Every time I taste a great wine–or wine that I think might be great–I ask myself, "How close does it come to being a perfect sphere?"

This, of course, is another way of asking: Does it have harmony? A wine that is harmonious has effectively corralled the various forces present in a wine—fruit, tannin, acidity, sweetness, alcohol—and managed to achieve a persuasive, cohesive whole. Harmony is the "dark matter" of wine, unseen and unmeasurable, yet somehow holding everything together.

In recent years, many tasters like to talk about "balance." That term gets trotted out whenever the issue of high alcohol in modern wines is either decried or defended. Detractors submit that such wines, which usually sail past the 15% alcohol mark, lack "balance." Defenders say that the measured alcohol is immaterial, as long as the wine has—you guessed it—"balance."

What are they talking about? Actually, it's quite simple—or rather, simplistic. Balance is the interrelation between fruit and acidity, as well as sweetness in a sweet wine. It's one element offsetting another, bringing it into, well, balance.

Although useful, "balance" inadvertently suggests a kind of precision, like a ballerina *en pointe*. The truth is that balance in wine is, instead, more a range of equivalencies, an approximate equilibrium of one force (fruit, acidity) offsetting the other.

"Balance" has become such a buzzword because high alcohol levels derived from ultra-ripe grapes add another element where buffering fruit offsets (and obscures) the otherwise likely "burn" of the high alcohol. Such big wines can attract stratospheric scores because they are dramatic. And they stand out in big tastings, never mind whether it's blind or not. A sizable number of wine drinkers—although far from all—find such high-alcohol wines bullying. "But they're not bullying if they are balanced," is the rejoinder.

Now you know why "balance" is such a potent term today. But is it sufficient? I would suggest not. "Harmonious" is a more comprehensive, nuanced notion. Far from suggesting a Lady Justice-like balancing scale where one thing merely offsets another, harmoniousness suggests the cohesive unity of the "perfect sphere."

Harmony inherently prizes inter-relation. Harmoniousness is not an end in itself, but rather, a beginning. Think of it as a chess game where no move is, or should be, evaluated merely on its own. Harmony is an attribute applicable to many things. A wine—or a dress, or a plate of food—must first be graceful and cohesive. Everything must work together, which is not the same as the boring uniformity of color coordination in clothes or a simplistic notion of offsets in a wine.

Various elements in a wine can only be judged in relation to their overall, interactive effect—which must be harmonious. Nothing can be out of whack. A wine cannot have too much mouth-rasping tannin. Or too little acidity. Then there is the quality and intensity of the fruit flavors. Sweetness adds its own element.

This interactive foundation to harmony calibrates your mind (and palate) to look for qualities that go well beyond "balance." This is why, collectively, women are better tasters than men (see page 96).

Women look at clothes and style not from a reductionist approach ("Those are beautiful shoes and they match the purse, therefore it's a great outfit"), but from a well-trained eye that sweeps across the entirety of the presentation and concludes that it either works or it somehow doesn't. And if it doesn't work, it's usually because of something to do with an absence of harmony. As the pianist Keith Jarrett once said, "I cannot say what I think is right about music. I only know the rightness of it."

At first, you would think that anything harmonious must somehow match (think "balance"). But it's not so. If anything, it's the opposite. Aesthetically, too much obvious coordination is boring. Nothing excites the

"*Harmony inherently prizes inter-relation. Think of it as a chess game where no move is, or should be, evaluated merely on its own. Everything must work together, which is not the same as the boring uniformity of color coordination in clothes or a simplistic notion of 'balance' or offsets in a wine.*"

eye. Or the palate. Or above all, the mind.

Part of our sense of harmony lies in our innate sense of the connectedness of things, the "rightness of it." This was explored by the Austrian philosopher Christian von Ehrenfels (1859-1932) who is credited today as one of the founders of what has come to be called gestalt psychology. Ehrenfels submitted that a melody consists of individual sounds, but that it is much more than the sum of these notes, pointing out that if we transpose the key we still always recognize the melody.

Referring to Ehrenfel's seminal thesis, *On the Qualities of Form* (1890), Rudolf Arnheim, a professor emeritus of the psychology of art at Harvard, notes that, "The appearance of any element depends on its place and function in an overall pattern."[4]

This is what makes harmony in a wine so essential. No great wine is actually "balanced." Instead, nearly every great wine offers a certain sort of originality that can be disturbing, or at least novel. Yet the wine's "dark matter" of harmony somehow holds it together.

The great Italian red wine, Barolo, made from the Nebbiolo grape variety, is a good example. Really, it tastes like nothing else except another Nebbiolo as its flavors are like no other, classically (and hardly attractively) described as an amalgam of *tar* and *roses*. Nebbiolo's acidity is among the highest of any red wine grape. And its tannins can be fierce. It's a beast of a grape yet somehow magical.

Upon tasting a Barolo (and many other easier but no less original-tasting great wines) you can find yourself echoing Francis Bacon, "If you examine it part by part, you shall find never a good; and yet altogether do well." How does it do that? You know the answer.

Without harmony holding all the elements together successfully, originality alone doesn't suffice. I've had wines with intriguing, highly original flavors but they also were heavy and over-extracted. They lacked cohesion. They jangled and fatigued your palate.

Harmony creates a sense of cohesion. Great wines are always somehow effortless. Flavors are beautifully defined; fruit and acidity, far from being "balanced," just flow seamlessly together—so much so that you don't even think about it. The wine practically floats. That's harmony.

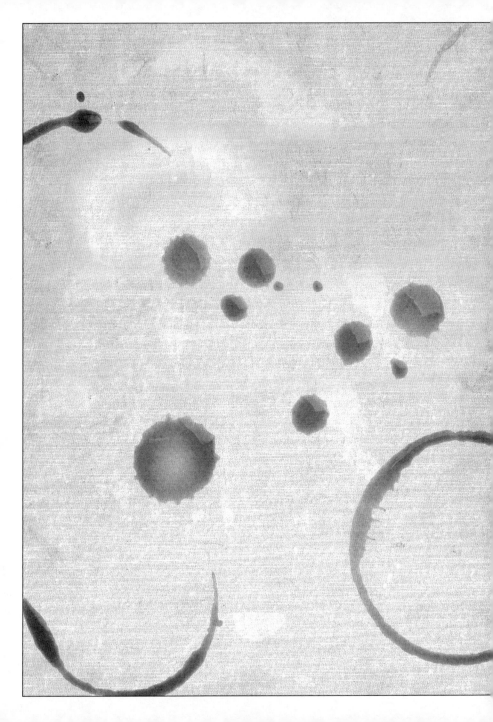

CHAPTER 4

TEXTURE

All I know is what I have words for.
—**Ludwig Wittgenstein,**
Philosophical Investigations (1953)

"Flavor descriptors are not really language. They are only terms of specificity without any inherent meaning. The important words about wines are those that lead us to what's actually meaningful in wine."

The challenge of wine is not, as many suppose, a matter of skill at tasting. Yes, it is essential to taste a lot wines and to think about what you're tasting. But the flavor identification acuity that so many people assume is the desideratum of wine tasting is misplaced. The real challenge of wine appreciation is not acuity but rather, an ability to speak insightfully about whatever it is that you may find in your glass.

This is why words matter. This is why flavor descriptors are–however odd this may sound–not really language. They are only terms of specificity without any inherent meaning. The important words about wines are those that lead us to what's actually meaningful in wine.

It's not a coincidence, for example, that French has an unusually rich and nuanced vocabulary of wine tasting terms. After all, a culture that has created as many great wines as France has cannot have done so without having devised a vocabulary that emphasizes and expresses the qualities being sought and achieved.

The English wine writer H. Warner Allen wrote in his quaintly titled book *The Romance of Wine* (1932) that, "One could wish that the words so badly needed by the wine-lover could be coined by some Lord of Language...and he might well begin by finding adequate translations for the shades of meaning expressed in French by such words as 'sève', 'finesse'..."

He has a point. Take the French word *sève* for example. Literally, it translates to "sap." But that definition hardly captures the quality that this significant term is trying to convey. The idea of *sève* is identifying textural density in wine–or its absence. The very existence of such a word signals how important French tasters thought that texture is in fine wine. A wine lacking *sève* is always considered lesser; one marks it down as "dilute" or "watery." It's a critical feature in fine wine everywhere.

For our part, we might choose simply to say "texture." However, the idea of *sève* is more than just texture, which is—for me, anyway—a broader, if still important, word. Keep in mind that texture can be enhanced in the winemaking process by various techniques.

If you were tasting with a winemaker he or she would likely use the term "mouth feel" to capture this. But that fails to direct one's attention to the source. You can enhance mouth feel by using a technique such as barrel fermenting, which is common with white wines. Fermenting a white wine in a small barrel, especially such varieties as Chardonnay and Sauvignon Blanc, gives it a thicker mouth feel. Barrel-fermenting can make a wine seem fuller, richer and denser. Is that "texture"? Sure it is. But only at the surface, as it were.

In comparison, "texture" is a broader term that captures a sense of fruit density, as well as the nature of the tannins in a red wine. As is well-known, tannins are frequently described as being ripe or green; coarse or fine-grained; gritty or silky. Obviously, the nature and quality of tannins will dramatically affect "texture," as will acidity. In white wines, the ratio of juice to skins can dramatically affect texture. Small berries with thick skins create very different wines. For example, the juice in white wines made from such tiny berries has a lot more pectin, which affects the texture of the resulting wine.

When you focus on texture you're going to look past flavor, sidestep youthful reticence and try to get a sense of potential depth. Texture helps tell the tale of a young wine's future or a mature wine's lost opportunity. Texture directs us to midpalate density, which is critical to a wine's potential depth over the long term, which is especially important in young wines hiding their flavor light under a bushel.

You can *feel* quality as well as taste it. In fact, you have to. Texture, as much as flavor, tells the tale.

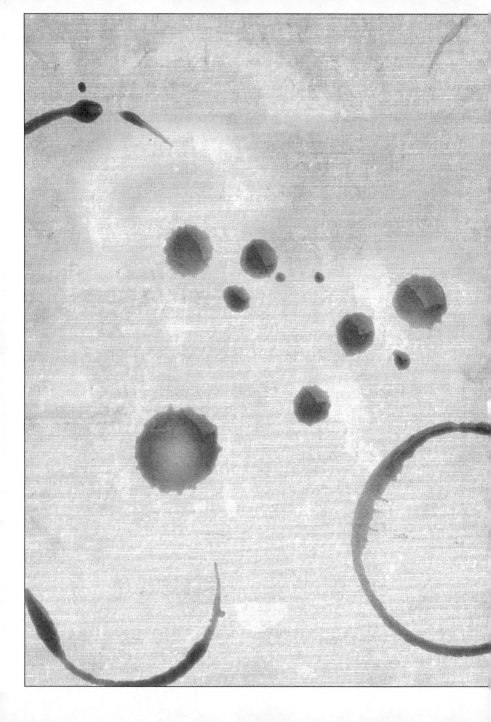

CHAPTER 5

LAYERS

A harmoniously conducted picture consists of a series of pictures superimposed on one another, each new layer conferring greater reality on the dream.

—Charles Baudelaire
Curiosités Ésthétiques (1868)

The most important question about wine is: What makes a wine good? The safe, populist answer is: If it tastes good to you, then it's good. That's also the worst possible answer. It's patronizing, an "everything will look better in the morning" reassurance for wine-drinking innocents.

So let's get to the nub of "good." "Good" exists independently of one's personal preference. How can this be? After all, isn't everything about wine subjective? So say the (often well-meaning) advisors who want to take snootiness out of wine. Ironically, such a notion about wine's purported snootiness is today more a knee-jerk reverse snobbery than anything resembling an accurate perception. Wine in the 21st century is now nearly as democratized as fast food, so ubiquitous and "normal" has it become.

But much about wine is anything but subjective. A great deal of our long-term, collective, cross-cultural appreciation about fundamental quality in wine—as opposed to style—is determined by our physiological and neurological makeup. This is no small thing and it goes a long way towards explaining why the "If you like it, it's good" mantra is nonsense.

What we like is just that, namely, preference. We've all got our preferences and, yes, we all have a right to our preferences. But just because something appeals doesn't make it good. Look at junk food. Even its admirers don't object to the name.

"Good" exists in matters of taste to the extent that we, as humans, have certain installed neurological and physiological predispositions. This is the key. Stripped to its structural skivvies, "good" for all of us humans works like this: We all have big brains and equally big cortexes. This is critical to understanding why "good" transcends taste or preference. Keep in mind that this same "good" can take many forms and tastes, some of which you or I may not like. But structurally, "good" always comes down to certain physiological and neurological fundamentals.

For example, decades of work in experimental psychology have demonstrated that our big brain/big cortex neurology seeks—"relishes" might be a better, if less scientific word—more complex stimuli over simpler stimuli. This is why we progress from "Mary Had A Little Lamb" to, say, Beethoven's Fifth Symphony. It's not just maturity that makes us say that Mary and her lamb are boring. It's that big cortex neurological need. It is simply a physiological fact that, over a period of time, we always seek more complex stimuli over simpler stimuli. We're set up that way.

Inevitably, the term conventionally—and not inaccurately—applied to this greater amount of stimuli is "complexity." There's nothing wrong with that word. It captures well enough the transition from, and difference between, simpler to, well... more complex. But I would suggest that, in terms of wine appreciation, a better description might be "layers."

The reason I propose "layers" is that a fully rewarding complexity is more than just multiplicity. It's not enough for a wine (or a painting or a piece of music) to have a lot going on. The trick—and it's no small trick, either—is that anything complex must simultaneously surprise us, and yet we must still be able to grasp these surprises as part of a larger and pleasing pattern. Here again, this is neurological in nature. Our brains insist upon finding patterns. We are set up to make sense of any jumble presented to us. And if we cannot find patterns we become irritated and fatigued.

This is one reason why Jackson Pollock's now-famous "drip" or "splatter" paintings so upset people when they first appeared, as well as long after. Never mind the lack of conventional artistry. What the hell does this incoherency *mean*? The apparent absence of cohesion was what really irritated. And if you read explications of Pollock's paintings, the central theme, the main defense, is that beneath the ostensible chaos there really *is* cohesion.[5]

The word "complexity" implicitly suggests that more is better. That's probably true, but how that "more" arrives to our senses is critical. We've all had wines with an almost explosive array of scents and tastes.

"It's not enough for a wine to have a lot going on. The trick— and it's no small trick, either—is that anything complex must simultaneously surprise us, and yet we must still be able to grasp these surprises as part of a larger and pleasing pattern."

We're wowed. "Boy, that's complex," we say.

But if you step back and ask yourself (and the wine) whether it has layers, you might well arrive at a different conclusion. You might find that, actually, there are no layers, or only a few. You might then conclude that its complexity is superficial rather than substantial and meaningful.

Such meaningful "complex" wines are, in my opinion, much better described as layered. The more you keep diving in, the more layers you pass through. Very great wines are seemingly bottomless. You keep passing through yet more layers, discovering something new and different.

This concept of layers helps serve to distinguish superficially complex wines, ones with a gaudy multiplicity, from the real thing. If you don't find layers, if that image doesn't readily come to mind when tasting a wine, chances are that a wine's seeming complexity is more makeup than substance. Here, semantics matters, if only as a means of distinguishing the cosmetic from the consequential.

Cosmetic complexity is more common than one might imagine thanks to a variety of winemaking techniques designed to give shallow wines an illusion of depth. You have, for example, various oak treatments that flavor a wine (different oaks, different degrees of "toast" or charring inside the barrel); barrel fermentation (which creates a thicker "mouth feel"); lees stirring (which imports flavor from the enzymatic breakdown of the yeasts); the use of vacuum concentrators (which removes water to make the wine more concentrated); and many other possibilities including additions, such as the use of wine concentrate to add flavor.

None of these, however, serve to create layers. Think bone structure compared to makeup. It must be noted, however, that looking for layers in very young wines can be difficult and sometimes impossible. This is why some wines wow critics and consumers upon release only to be tasted years later and found disappointing. No wine taster is exempt from such errors of judgment, especially in today's rushed wine tasting environment where hundreds of wines are tasted over relatively short time span.

But the fact that very young wines may not, in their extreme youth, reveal layers should not deter tasters for looking for them. It's the search that matters, as it focuses one's tasting attention on features, such as texture, that at least promise the possibility of layers.

To ask for "complexity" is to ask only for a sense of kaleidoscopic variety, an iridescent sheen on the surface of a wine. To ask for layers is to seek much more than the dazzle of variety. It emphasizes instead a search for a sense of depth...*each new layer conferring greater reality on the dream.*

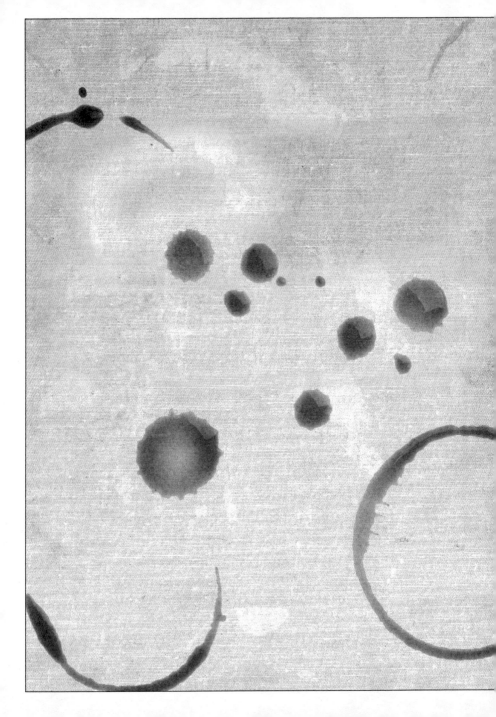

CHAPTER 6

FINESSE

It's more of a finesse game, it's more small ball, which personally I don't really care much for. I like kind of smash-mouth, old-school basketball.

—Kobe Bryant
Los Angeles Times

It's not a coincidence that, with the possible exception of tennis, no sport sees the word "finesse" invoked more often than basketball. And even though I'm no sports fan myself, I have found basketball imagery one of the most effective in conveying at least a visual notion of finesse.

What is finesse in wine? It's one of those "you know it when you see it" things—or in this case, taste it. Finesse is about delivery, how a wine's flavors and texture are handed to you. Think of a basketball player going for a layup. Finesse is when the player is driving toward the basket, gracefully leaping up with the ball rolling off his fingertips and disappearing friction-free into the basket. The same play can, of course, be done brutally: the slam dunk. No one has ever suggested that as having finesse.

Fine wine isn't, however, a matter of getting a ball through a hoop, of winning or losing, never mind how. That's why finesse matters so much in wine and so little in sports. Wine is an end in itself; there is no finish line to cross. In sports, finesse is an added bonus, a fillip of graceful beauty in movement and skill. With wine, finesse is intrinsic to full accomplishment.

Clearly, the word *finesse* is a Frenchified version of fine-ness. This alone tells you how structurally important finesse is in establishing the refinement of a wine. No one has ever praised a wine for being coarse.

Granted, establishing finesse is a matter of judgment and far from an exact science. Indeed, it can't be measured, which is why wine scientists scorn the very idea of finesse.

Finesse is like the Shaolin priest in *Kung Fu* who, "looked for, he cannot be seen. Felt, he cannot be touched." In other words, finesse cannot be rationally proved as real. No winemaking technique insures finesse. This drives the "causality crowd" crazy. Consequently, wine scientists have banned both the concept and the term itself. "This word [finesse] needs a rest, along with 'delicate' and 'elegant,'" wrote professors Maynard Amerine and Edward B. Roessler in *Wines: Their Sensory Evaluation*.[6] This is a willfully blindered view of quality in wine, a form of narrow-mindedness justified by an abiding belief in scientism.

Well, they work their side of the street and wine lovers—connoisseurs, really—work theirs. Finesse exists. It's real. And not only does it exist, but what's more, finesse is an foundational element of *all* truly great wines anywhere in the world regardless of grape variety or style.

If we proscribe the word *finesse* as part of our wine vocabulary we do so at genuine risk. "To name a thing is to make it real," said Albert Camus (it's attributed to him, anyway). Wine values, like any others, lose their life essence if not invoked. Finesse will become less important if it's never mentioned. Which wine world would you prefer to live in? One where finesse is sought and its absence duly noted? Or one where *toasty oak* dominates the discussion?

Yes, fashion plays a role. The taste of one era or culture can choose to prize finesse or ignore it. But centuries of fine-wine appreciation suggest that, over time, after a culture has rung its changes in taste from preferring something powerful and unsubtle to wines that are more restrained and polished, finesse emerges as a critical marker of refinement. This has occurred everywhere, by the way. France had several such moments over the centuries, as did England, Italy, Spain and Portugal. California and Australia are currently in the throes of just such a phase, although a preference for power in wine in both places is now far from as monolithic as it once was.

Today, as previously mentioned, there's a fierce debate about whether modern wines are excessively alcoholic. Such wines are said to "taste well," but not "drink well." They are slam-dunk wines: exciting, showy and "smash-mouth." They are said to lack finesse.

Is it true? Hard to say. Some of today's wines are indeed guilty, while others are innocent of the accusation. In basketball, even a 300-pound center can score with finesse. Big wines don't necessarily have to be brutes.

Still, it sometimes feels, *à la* Kobe Bryant, that the wine world is divided between "smash-mouth" and "small ball." Popular thinking has it that, depending upon your emotional needs and stylistic preferences, you're either an adherent to finesse in wine or you seek a smash-mouth flavor impact and to hell with finesse.

Real quality arrives in many guises. Alcohol level alone tells us almost nothing about wine quality. I've had lovely wines that had alcohol as low as five to seven percent by volume (Moscato d'Asti or German Riesling, for example) or as high as sixteen or seventeen percent (Zinfandel, Grenache, Recioto della Valpolicella Amarone). High alcohol levels do unquestionably make finesse harder to achieve, but hardly preclude it.

That acknowledged, let me also acknowledge something else: most higher-alcohol wines, in my experience, usually *do* fail to achieve or offer finesse. This not because of high alcohol (typically 15 percent or more) in isolation, but because of what created the high alcohol to begin with, namely, overripeness at harvest. Like telling a fat man to cut down on eating ice cream, alcohol is just a symptom; *excess* is the heart of it.

Wines made from overripe grapes too often lack refreshing acidity. Overripe fruit in wine too often is not just big, but bullying in its declaration. Delicacy is lost. High alcohol is just one of several forces that combine to make a wine overbearing and clumsy, no matter how initially showy or dramatic.

But what about those high-alcohol wines that *are* successful? What saves them from the abyss? Several sources can confer grace on these heavyweights: cool climate, especially in autumn and at night during the growing season; soil (typically very stony) or sometimes just the vagary of a particular vintage. Such wines manage to retain a full measure of apparent acidity (which is not just what's measured but what you actually detect as a taster), and—this is critical—their fruit does not taste overripe.

Remember, sugars can increase—which in turn creates the higher alcohol—without a corresponding increase in pruney/raisiny overripeness. Typically this is from cooling autumn days and even cooler nighttime temperatures which preserve acidity and slow the dehydration which can accompany overripeness. (Many wines picked at high sugar levels, measured in degrees Brix—a grape at 28 degrees Brix creates a wine with approximately 15.5 percent alcohol—are "watered down" with water added to replace what was lost from dehydration.)

This is why there are higher-alcohol wines that are successful. This is why focusing on alcohol content alone begs the question. This is why focusing on finesse is revealing. Successful higher-alcohol wines have it. Unsuccessful ones do not.

"Finesse is when the wine does all the work, as it serves to effortlessly deliver all the forces present in the wine to you. It presents these without your having to either look for them or somehow sidestep them. A wine with finesse always seems subtle, no matter how big or powerful."

This also underscores why finesse is such a vital, irreplaceable value. If you prize finesse in a wine, if you seek it in what you choose to buy, then what you esteem in wine necessarily changes. The very search for finesse alters everything. If winemakers, for their part, truly prized finesse as an essential attribute in fine wine, there is no way—I mean *no way*—that they would issue many of the wines they put on the market today. Indeed, they might not even plant their vines in certain locales for that same reason.

The same must also be said of wine tasters. If finesse was a high-value feature of their aesthetic "pyramid," there similarly would be no way that they would heap praise and high scores on wines that are not merely higher in alcohol but are so obviously overripe in flavor and clumsy in delivery. A reverence for finesse effectively precludes such wines from praise and validation.

Since finesse is about delivery, it's easily understood why a lighter-weight wine can more easily achieve finesse than a stronger and heavier wine. That noted, when a more powerful wine does manage to deliver itself to us with uncommon grace and seeming ease—in other words, finesse—it can rightly be highly praised as a remarkable accomplishment. This is why the great red Bordeaux have achieved their prices and reputation. This is why the best Australian Shiraz wines can be so impressive; many of them are big and yet the best

Australian Shirazes do indeed have finesse. Not least, the same may be said of California's best Cabernet Sauvignons. A great California Cabernet is a marvel of density and intensity allied to finesse.

With that in mind, wines of finesse tend to come from one or more of the following circumstances:

Cooler climates which allow for flavor development over a long growing season without accompanying high sugar content can create wines of finesse more readily than warmer climates. More than any other single factor, cool climate grape-growing is a means towards a likely end result of finesse.

Grape varieties with higher than usual levels of acidity, such as Nebbiolo, Barbera, Pinot Noir and Riesling, tend to display more finesse than wines with lower inherent acidity. Acidity is a key to finesse. No wine described as "flabby" could possibly be declared as also having finesse.

Grapes grown on certain soils, especially chalk, schist and granite, tend to have more finesse than grapes grown on heavier soils, such as clay. This, however, cannot be viewed in isolation, as the coolness (or warmth) of the climate during the growing season is so influential. A cool climate coupled with such soils almost guarantees wines with uncommon finesse.

Wines made with techniques that do not emphasize extreme flavor or color extraction, such as extended cold maceration, will more likely display finesse than those subjected to such techniques.

Wines that are not handled in such a way as to add more flavors through the use of heavy toast oak or extended lees stirring are more likely to display finesse than wines made with intrusive, flavor-modifying techniques. Here again, if the grapes are grown in a cool climate on, say, chalky soils, these techniques do not necessarily preclude finesse.

Finesse is when the wine does all the work, as it serves to effortlessly deliver all the forces present in the wine to you. It presents these without your having to either look for them or somehow sidestep them. One key is this: A wine with finesse always seems subtle, no matter how big or powerful.

A marker of finesse is an absence of fatigue. Inevitably, finesse does not exist independently of other qualities in the wine, especially harmoniousness. Although I suppose it's possible, I'm hard-pressed to think of an example of wine that lacked harmony and yet still had finesse.

Also, it's worth mentioning that although delicacy is incontestably a handmaiden to finesse, delicacy alone does not guarantee finesse. After all, delicacy can be achieved by sheer lightness, without much depth of flavor or character requiring or demonstrating the presence of finesse.

Finesse buoys both a wine and its taster. If, when you are drinking a wine (as opposed to a quick sip-and-spit tasting), you find yourself growing weary, that's a good sign that a wine lacks finesse.

There's no question that restraint or austerity in winemaking furthers the cause of finesse. A wine with big, obvious, gloopy fruit will never have finesse. It can't. A degree of restraint, either intrinsic to the fruit itself or imparted to it by careful winemaking, is a prerequisite.

When wines are like a great oration where you're carried along, feeling like you understand everything effortlessly, that's finesse.

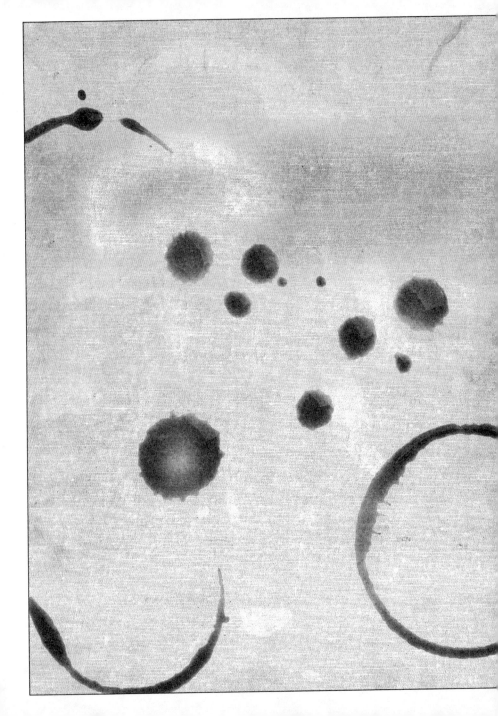

CHAPTER 7

SURPRISE

A school-master of mine long ago said, "You can only learn from the second-raters. The first-raters are out of range; you can't see how they get their effects."

—Raymond Chandler
Selected Letters of Raymond Chandler

Surprise is the secret sauce of great wine. Indeed, if you want to know if a wine really is "great" look for the element of surprise. If it's not there, it's not great.

Surprise is another way of saying "originality." But that term, although fair and useful, is so eroded by promiscuous use that it no longer registers. Anything that anyone likes is given the accolade of "original," never mind whether it truly is or not. (Its cloying rival in overuse is "special.")

Surprise puts a finger on what, in fact, makes something original. Originality is more than a matter of not resembling anything else. While that's true as far as it goes, in the case of fine wine, it doesn't go much of a distance. If Leo Tolstoy was a wine lover he might well have put it this way: All unsurprising wines are alike; each wine of surprise is surprising in its own way. This is true originality. It is a kind of unpredictability, even when you think you know what you're likely to get.

This was brought home to me on a subject far removed from wine. It involved Frank Sinatra. For many years I was unmoved by Sinatra's singing. The only Sinatra I originally knew was the "Rat Pack" version and that lounge lizardry hardly revealed the mastery, indeed the uniqueness, of his art.

Anyway, later in life I became friends with Baylor Lowes who participated in my wine tasting classes and was a full generation older than I. Over a long span of years we had lunch together nearly every Friday afternoon. Our conversations ranged over many subjects. I knew about wine and food; Bay, as a former banker, knew the psychology and reality of money, about which I was hopelessly ignorant. (So much for a liberal arts education.) He also knew a lot about Frank Sinatra's music and slowly, patiently, brought me around to recognize and appreciate that Sinatra really was *sui generis*.

I mention this because of a deceptively simple yet penetrating observation he made about Sinatra's singing: You can't sing along with him. "Everybody talks about the beauty of his voice and, especially, his phrasing," said Bay. "But that begs the question. What was it that made the phrasing so memorable?"

"That's what made Sinatra so different," he continued. "You discover listening to a standard you've heard a million times before that, wherever you imagine or expect he's going with the next note, the next syllable or the next phrase, you're wrong. That's what makes Sinatra's singing and his famous phrasing unique. There's always that surprise."

I've tested my friend's assertion hundreds of times since then, and he's right. Unless you've memorized exactly how Sinatra sang a certain song, you really cannot sing along with him; you can't intuit where's he's going. Try it and you'll agree for yourself.

This is consistent with the much more abstract the-

"Real surprise comes from expectations that are simultaneously first generated, then violated and finally confirmed again. This is what happens when we drink great wines. This is why we linger over such wines. We keep coming back for more, in the scent, in the taste, in the aftertaste. We certainly get a sense of layers. But each layer is its own surprise."

ories of information theory. According to the philosopher and composer Leonard B. Meyer (1918-2007), complexity in music is uncertainty.[7] We have, *à la* Sinatra, expectations which are aroused, fulfilled or frustrated. What we tease out of this uncertainty is "meaning." Put another way, surprise creates a sense of difference, of originality.

Philosophers also point to the element of tension or suspense. Aaron Smuts in the *Stanford Encyclopedia of Philosophy* asks, "If uncertainty is required in order for one to feel suspense, then how is it that some narrative artworks can still seem suspenseful on repeated encounters?" This problem is known as the *paradox of suspense.* If suspense requires uncertainty and yet we already know how the story—a book, a movie, a piece of music or even a wine—ends, why then do we nevertheless feel suspense even though we already know how it ends?

Theories abound, none of them conclusive. One of them involves the element of surprise which, at a deeper level yet, is based on the foundation of "expectation." Simply put, much of our sensation of surprise comes from expectation. Matthew M. Lavy, a philosopher at the University of Cambridge, submits: "Meyer's theory of expectation in western tonal music—that expectations are perpetually generated then violated or confirmed as the music unfolds—is essentially a theory of how the structure of western music helps a listener create a narrative experience."[8]

It's easy to get lost in all these theories about how we seek surprise and what makes us repeatedly surprised. That it applies to wine is likely itself a surprise to some, but it's so. Truly fine wine offers us a narrative of sorts. We taste, then re-taste, then taste yet again. Wines of originality/surprise keep spinning out their tale, as it were. A great wine is a Scheherazade: we are transfixed by its seemingly endless series of suspenseful chapters.

This is why, and how, wine lovers can say that one wine is greater than another. A frequently-voiced skepticism—a populist petulance, really—is: Who are *you* to say that one wine is better than another? Well, that's the point. It's not a matter of what you or I say. It's a matter of what the *wine* says. Since we're neurologically predisposed toward complexity/uncertainty/surprise, the hierarchy of better or less good has already been predetermined. A wine that continually surprises us in a pleasing cohesive fashion—a narrative, if you like—is better than one that doesn't. If you don't like that, well then, take it up with the Creator. This is how we are wired.

This is also why certain grape varieties are also considered superior to others, never mind your or my taste preferences. Nebbiolo, *as a grape variety*, is always better than Barbera. Of course a good Barbera trumps a bad Nebbiolo any time. But the capacity of Nebbiolo as a grape for offering us a "narrative" of layers and harmony and continuing surprise is inherently superior to that of Barbera. (For the record, it so happens that I reach for a really good Barbera much more often than I do Nebbiolo, in the same way that I listen to Frank Sinatra or chamber music more than Mahler's symphonies.)

Now, with a group of wines that we can all agree are pretty much equally surprising, and thus original, then it really does become a matter of taste. With such equality one has every right and reason to reject the notion that one wine is better than another.

Surprise, rather than unusual taste, is what makes wines original. This is why first impressions most definitely do not count in the world of fine wine. After all, if you've never previously tasted a Greek Assyrtiko (a white grape variety) or a South African Pinotage (a red grape crossing of Pinot Noir and Cinsault) you might say that you're "surprised," as they taste different from more commonly-experienced wines.

But that's not surprise. It's just unfamiliarity. Real surprise comes, as Leonard Meyer pointed out, from expectations that are simultaneously first generated, then violated and finally confirmed again. Think of a kaleidoscope where, as you turn the cylinder, patterns are created, then disturbed and then a new, equally rewarding pattern reappears.

This is what happens when we drink great wines. This is why we linger over such wines. They are almost too much. But not quite. They don't overwhelm so much as endlessly tease and seduce (surprise again). We keep coming back for more, in the scent, in the taste, in the aftertaste. We certainly get a sense of layers. But each layer is its own surprise.

In this regard the acclamation of a wine as "great" reflects a consensus. Generations of tasters, often from a variety of nationalities and cultures, repeatedly and delightedly find "surprise" in such wines, even when they've had them across a variety of vintages. They know what's coming, and yet the wine continues to intrigue every time.

What's more, the bone-deep element of surprise/originality in great wines seems to transcend winemaking technique. For example, I'm always struck by the fact that nearly all of the red Burgundies acclaimed today were originally what we would unhesitatingly now consider a *rosé*. Red wines as we know them are created by a prolonged mingling of pigment-rich skins with the juice. (Nearly all grapes have colorless juice.) To do this requires large vats or casks, as the skins are bulky.

When you look at wine harvest scenes in French tapestries from the 1400s, however, you don't see any large fermenting vats. That's because they didn't appear until the 1600s. And even then, the vats were not often used for what the French call *cuvaison*, which is the process of allowing the juice of red grapes to ferment with the skins.

Even as late as 1807, when truly red Burgundies appeared, the French minister of agriculture, Jean-Antoine Chaptal, described Burgundy's still-traditional method of fermentation: "Lighter wines of Burgundy can't take more than six to 12 hours of *cuvaison*. The most famous of these is Volnay. This wine, so fine, so delicate, so agreeable, can't stand a *cuvaison* of more than 18 hours and doesn't last from one harvest to the next." It was a *rosé*, pure and apparently not so simple. Here's the thing: By 1807 nearly every significant *premier* and *grand cru* vineyard in Burgundy had already been identified and qualitatively judged.

Our wine-loving forebears could hear volumes in a mere whisper. We will never experience the antique insight of, say, a Richebourg *rosé*, even if we could taste one today. Their sensory world was calibrated differently from ours. Light was not slight to them. But for the reasons previously noted, they, too, felt the gratification of surprise. And when a certain site delivered it consistently they called it *terroir*—which is really just a one-word way of declaring "*the surprise is always there.*" Great *terroir* is a spring of surprise that never dries up.

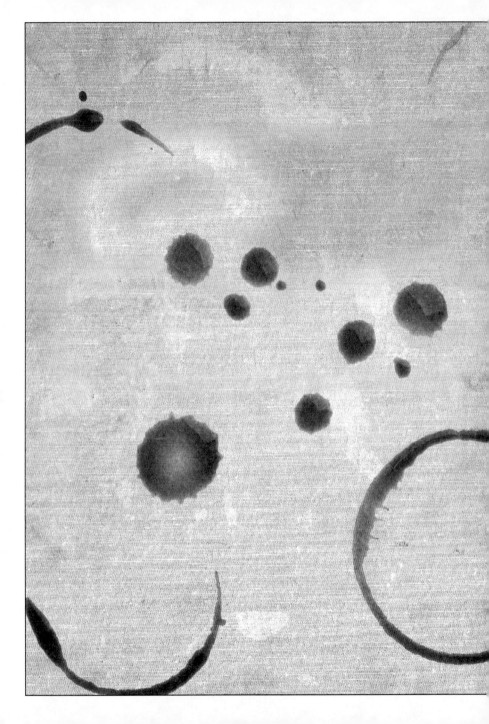

CHAPTER 8

NUANCE

Did you notice her eyebrows?

—Karen Kramer

Of all the words that, Ouija-like, will move your taste in one direction or another, it's "nuance." If nuance is an attribute that you prize—and I most definitely think that you should—then you will choose and value certain sorts of wines. If nuance is something you either cannot credit or just flat-out reject, then you can be certain that your taste in wine will assuredly head in a very different direction.

Here we come to the crux of the matter: Without nuance a wine has no shadings, no subtleties, no layered depths. Whatever lingering, repeated, absorbed attention you find yourself paying to a wine is because of nuance. (That said, it must be admitted that a high price, like a hanging, also has a way of focusing attention). If there are few dark corners to a wine, no intimation of secrets, your attention wavers after a few sniffs and sips; then it departs altogether. You either then continue to drink unthinkingly or push it away in search of something more intriguing.

Nuance is all about shadings and details. Paying attention to such details requires, in turn, a certain amount of training. This is why, especially in the early stages of wine appreciation, women are indisputably better than men at wine tasting.

I'm a guy so I can say it: In matters of nuance most men are dolts. It's not a chromosomal thing. There's nothing about how either men and women are genetically constructed that gives women a clear edge in wine tasting, the media hoopla about "supertasters" notwithstanding.[9] Scientists have shown that there *are* differences between women and men in our ability to taste, with women having an edge. But those differences mostly center on sensitivities or insensitivities to particular tastes or scents and vary from culture to culture, as well as among age groups.

"In general, women have a keener sense of smell than men, and older people regain their olfactory capacity less quickly than younger people after an 'olfactory bombardment'," says Piet Vroon in *Smell: The Secret Seducer* (1997). Scientists are only in the early stages of sorting out the many inconsistencies in the human ability to distinguish and identify scents and odors, as Piet Vroon notes:

"Research is further complicated by the fact that people display wide differences both in their sensitivity to smells and in their appreciation of smells.... Even among normal, healthy people the sense of smell varies enormously...Moreover, depending on the circumstances there is also a great deal of variation within the same individual: one processes the smell of fried eggs differently the morning after a drinking binge than on the evening of the same day after a healthy ramble through the woods."

The broad scientific brushstroke is that we all have

strengths and weaknesses in our ability to detect scents and odors at differing thresholds. Overall, women are indeed better at smelling things than are men.

Now, for the non-scientific perspective: What women are really better at is *noticing* what they are smelling. They pay more attention—and they value what results from that attentiveness. I've taught wine-tasting classes for decades and, like a lot of others, I've seen women taste wine "better" than men. This is especially so at the novice level and, in my observation, the difference diminishes as everyone becomes more experienced and—a critical point—is equally willing to pay attention.

This brings me to the key word about nuance: eyebrows. When I've voiced that very sentence in speaking engagements and wine-tasting classes the universal reaction (quite understandably) is puzzlement. What do eyebrows have to do with wine? Obviously, they have nothing to do with wine. But as an illustrative lesson they have everything to do with understanding nuance.

Every woman I know has been trained from a very early age to pay attention to appearance and, especially, clothes. Now, whether they choose to pursue this ardently as adults depends upon the individual. But I've yet to meet a woman who has not been "trained" by their mothers, aunts, girlfriends, magazines, newspapers, movies, clerks at makeup counters in department stores and I don't know where else, about the ever-finer matters of making oneself attractive.

This is an alien universe for the great majority of men. We're out of it, in every sense. We know only one way to knot a tie and—if we're even still wearing a tie these days—that's the knot we use for the rest of our lives. Ever watch a guy decide which tie goes with which shirt? It's not a pretty sight. Once we land on a combination that meets approval (typically from our wives or girlfriends) we stay with it without additional thought or even much interest.

Compare that with what girls and women engage in: fabrics, texture, colors, lengths, hairstyles, hair colors, makeup, scents, accessories, shoe styles, heel height and I don't know what else. It's a dizzying cascade of choices, all connected. The color is right, but the texture is wrong; these shoes don't work with that dress, and so forth.

Over decades this instruction on how to deal with these daily challenges pours in from all sides. Often it's conflicting: Your mother disapproves, but the fashionistas say it's the chic thing. Every woman knows all about this. They learn to sort it all out for themselves. We men are oblivious.

Anyway, my wife, Karen, and I were walking down the street. Coming at us from the opposite direction

"The necessity of nuance is a matter of sustaining your interest. No single feature, even those as essential as layers and harmony and finesse, is sufficient. It's nuance that seduces. It's nuance that keeps you coming back. Strident wines soon become fatiguing, however impactful their first impression. Nuance is the necessary shade to their sunshine. It offers both relief and contrast."

was a well-dressed woman who, I must say, certainly caught my eye. After she passed by, Karen turned to me and asked if I had seen her. I replied, as coolly as I could that, why yes, as I matter of fact I did.

"Did you notice her eyebrows?"

At that moment, I was flabbergasted. I mean, I don't think there's a guy alive—apart from makeup artists and the like—who pays any attention to a woman's *eyebrows*. "I barely got above the neck," I confessed. Karen ignored that and intoned, "The eyebrows frame the face."

I have since run that "eyebrows frame the face" line past dozens of women and the response was, without exception, "Well, of course." *Eyebrows frame the face.* I have yet to hear of any guy having an eyebrow fetish. But plenty of women apparently have one. I had no idea how much attention gets paid to eyebrows by women.

This was one of the great wine lessons of my life. I'm not kidding. Any group that has reached a level of aesthetic analysis that pays such a degree of attention to something as seemingly minor (but apparently not really) as eyebrows knows *all* about nuance. Not just its existence, mind you, but also its importance.

This is why I've previously declared that if you give me a class of wine novices, all of whom are women, I can take them three times further in wine appreciation than I can a group of men. Scientists can say what they like about physiological differences between the sexes. I know better: it's eyebrows.

Now, we men *can* learn about nuance, and many of us have. In my wine-tasting classes I use sports analogies, and most guys then get it. It's what *we've* been "trained" to. But learning to prize nuance, well, that's something else again. That's where women are way ahead of men. It's a divide that, although easily enough bridged, does take some willingness if, unlike girls and women, you're not previously instructed to its presence and credit its importance.[10]

Are there cultural differences in play as well, never mind gender? You bet there are. It's no coincidence that both American and Australian wine drinkers and wine producers alike have long prized powerful wines. Many still do, although the iron grip of that preference is weakening. Even boosters of both cultures—and I enthusiastically count myself among them—cannot deny that both Australia and the United States are young nations with histories of facing formidable natural challenges (continental scale, drought, fierce or venomous critters) with fortitude and obstinance. No wonder each culture prized forthrightness over subtlety and—you guessed it—nuance.

All that is changing, of course. In creating fine wine you cannot go beyond your culture. Twenty-first century Australia[11] and America[12] alike are rapidly transforming from swill-it-and-kill-it beer cultures to—dare I say it?—more refined wine cultures. It hardly needs to be pointed out that Italy and, especially, France long ago recognized and embraced the role and importance of nuance in so many aspects of their respective civilizations.

Nuance is not, as some might presume, merely a matter of delicacy. Big wines can have nuance. Nuance requires layers. It requires a refreshing acidity and an absence of excessive, coarse tannins. There must be harmony with all of the forces in the wine. This is harder for large-scale wines (Australian Shiraz, many California Cabernets, Portuguese reds, Barolo) to achieve, but by no means impossible. Ironically, it takes nuance to create nuance—choosing your picking times, your winemaking techniques, as well as selecting a site that itself has it own nuance.

This last point may sound odd or even ridiculous. It's not. Until very recently in the long history of wine, growers pursued almost no intervention in the vineyard itself. The big choice was which grape varieties to plant and when to harvest. There was no irrigation, as is so common today. At most, growers added a little fertilizer and restored topsoil from hillsides that experienced runoff after a bad storm or a harsh winter.

The great vineyard sites of Europe proved, over centuries, to be themselves creatures of nuance, a natural conjunction of climate, soil, exposure and rainfall that, through the revelation of the right grape, proved to be unique. The French chose to call this nuanced complexity and subtlety *terroir*. But it's hardly confined to France. Indeed, all great wines, regardless of grape variety, come from sites of nuance.

I'll always remember walking in Napa Valley's famed To-Kalon Vineyard, which was first created in 1866 by Hiram Crabb. As most of it is today owned by the Robert Mondavi Winery, I was accompanied by one of Mondavi's vineyard managers. It was a hot summer day.

Most significantly, it was the second year of a two-year drought that had everyone wringing their hands about a reduction of water for irrigation and the long-term demise of winegrowing in California. (California is prone to droughts; no sooner does one end and everyone promptly forgets, and then another arrives, and you're sure to read the same apocalyptic reports all over again.)

As we walked through the lush, verdant To-Kalon Vineyard it suddenly dawned on me that there were no overhead sprinklers nor drip emitters on the ground. There was no irrigation. Everywhere else, vine leaves were curling and browning from the lack of water and the summer's heat. Not here.

"There's no irrigation." I exclaimed in wonderment. "No need," laconically replied the vineyard manager.

When I pressed him for a reason why, he shrugged and called it the "power of the land." "We've never had irrigation," he added. "Never needed it."

"There's something about the site," he continued. "It occupies a kind of nexus where we get the right temperature and the right soil and subsoil and the right amount of water which slides in underground from the Mayacamas Mountains you can see to the west of us. It's held in the subsoil here. I'd love to take credit for it, but I can't," he added. "It's a very particular spot."

If that isn't nuance, I don't know what is. Does it translate to the wine? It sure does—at least if the right grape varieties are planted and the vineyard management (trellising, pruning, yields, picking times) and winemaking are also suitably nuanced and competent.

The more you visit the vineyards that create the world's greatest wines, the more you hear variations of the same story. The French writer Colette called it "celestial wizardry." Every great vineyard site has its particular tale of challenges overcome—heat, water, elevation, slope, soils—but once human ingenuity has maneuvered around them by using terraces or irrigation or drainage or just sheer stubbornness, the eventual uniqueness that created such a great wine is acknowledged by the growers to be something well beyond their human achievement. It's a nuance of site, one irreproducible anywhere else, even right next door.

From a wine drinking point of view the necessity of nuance is a matter of sustaining your interest. No single feature, even those as essential as layers and harmony and finesse, is sufficient. It's nuance that seduces. It's nuance that keeps you coming back. Strident wines soon become fatiguing, however impactful their first impression. Nuance is the necessary shade to their sunshine. It offers both relief and contrast.

This is why nuance is always found in all of the world's finest wines. It alone allows you to feel as if you're exploring the wine, like looking at a sculpture from all angles, circling it and seeing new features, thanks to different shadings. Without nuance it's all glare and blare.

Of all the essential features of great wine, nuance is the one most challenged in today's wine environment. One reason is that so many wines now are judged (and often dismissed) when they are very young. Only rarely does nuance make itself known in very young wines.

Also, because so many wines are now judged in large groupings, it's impossible for fine shadings to be appreciated. Recognizing nuance takes time; one must linger over a glass, a bottle, preferably during the course of a meal. The proof of this is found in a refrain that wine lovers have voiced for centuries and still do today: "The last glass was simply so good."

This "last glass" phenomenon is real. Yes, partly it's

due to the increased exposure to air that a bottle of wine receives as it sits on the table over the course of a meal. Science would have you believe, with reason (in every sense) that the "last glass" phenomenon is a function of oxidation. That's surely true. But it fails to capture the critical role of nuance. After all, if the wine, however complex, just kept blaring at you from the start of the meal to the end, the "last glass" phenomenon wouldn't exist. It's the shadings of nuance that create that "last glass" longing, that sense of having discovered features to a wine only at the very end of the experience.

Nuance takes time. The wine itself needs time in the form of aging. The drinker needs time to get past the exterior beauty of a striking wine (including its label) and find its interior beauty. Nuance, in the end, is all about interior beauty.

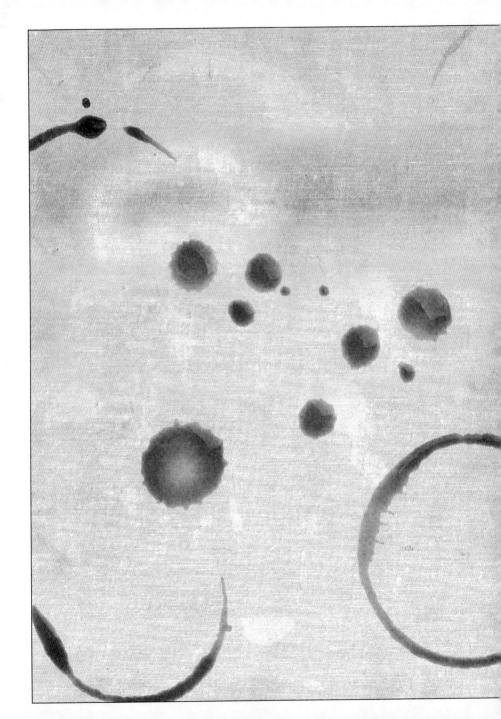

A WORD ABOUT NUANCE AND CHEESE

Cheese is eaten with red wine, pure and simple.

—Pierre Androuët
Guide du Fromage (1973)

The matter of nuance in wine is never more apparent than when cheese comes into the picture. The pairing of wine and cheese is more than famous; it is symbolic and powerfully evocative. Traditionally, the wine has always been red, as the famous Parisian cheese merchant, Pierre Androuët so definitively declared.

This impression that red wine is the ideal pairing with cheese persists to this day. Does it work? Of course it does, with the obvious acknowledgment that much inevitably depends upon the cheese. With many hundreds of cheeses to choose from, it's absurd, *pace* Pierre Androuët, to declare red wine the champion partner for every cheese.

But what is forgotten about the venerable "red wine with cheese" prescription is that it actually applies *less* today than ever before. The reason involves nuance. Simply put, the red wines we drink today aren't anywhere near as well-aged as those enjoyed when the red-wine-with-cheese dictum was universally accepted.

Prior to the mid-20th-century—and especially before World War I—wine lovers wouldn't dream of drinking a red wine that didn't have at least 20 years of age on it. Many red Bordeaux didn't even appear on the market until a decade after the vintage. And good merchants would often cellar them for yet another 10 years.

This is tellingly conveyed by the observations of the British writer P. Morton Shand (1888-1960) in a chapter added decades later to his *A Book of French Wines* (1928). An upper class Englishman down to his polished Lobb boots (schooled at Eton and King's College, Cambridge), Shand was an astute and acerbic writer who both witnessed and spanned the divide between wine as it was made and enjoyed in the Edwardian era and the beginnings of contemporary wine modernity.

In the revised *A Book of French Wines* (1960), a new chapter titled "Changed Tastes In Wine" captures the change from 1928 when the book first appeared: "Before we were halfway between the two World Wars people in Britain were already becoming accustomed... to consuming what up to the First World War would have been dismissed with astonishment as barbarously raw or unwholesomely immature wines."

After pointing out the economic causes for this circumstance, Shand delved deeper yet. "I realized a definite shift in taste must be setting in when I found men of riper years who prided themselves on keeping up with the times had suddenly discovered extraordinary virtues in wines of extreme youth: Virtues, they would solemnly assure one, which were inevitably lost with bottle-age."

Such aged red wines are much more delicately fruity and consequently more deferential to cheese than today's bold red wines served with a mere few year's worth of aging.

"Too many red wines today are simply too big, too bold and too young—too lacking in nuance, in other words—to successfully consort with many cheeses. Obviously, exceptions abound, as there are simply so many wines and cheeses to choose from. But the generalization is nevertheless both defensible and valid."

Not only has the amount of aging been reduced from spans once counted in decades to mere years today, if that, but the winemaking has changed equally as dramatically. For example, prior to the 1970s a high-end red Bordeaux, one of the famous *crus classés* or classed growths such as Château Lafite-Rothschild or the like, typically offered an alcohol level of just 10 percent or 11 percent. Today, the same wines never dip below 13 percent alcohol and can easily show up with 14 percent or even more.

While modern red Bordeaux can be as great, or greater, than the now-legendary old versions, there's no question that today's red Bordeaux—and every other red wine everywhere in the world—is more deeply colored, richer and bolder than its predecessors. Technology has changed; tastes have changed. (Shand, for his part, diagnosed the cause to the hurriedness of the age: "The strain and competitive haste of post-war life bred an impatience to enjoy." And that was in 1960. One can only imagine what he would have thought of today's hyper-accelerated pace.)

All of which brings us back to the specific matter of cheese and nuance. Too many red wines today are simply too big, too bold and too young—too lacking in nuance, in other words—to successfully consort with many cheeses. Obviously, exceptions abound, as there are simply so many wines and cheeses to choose from.

But the generalization is nevertheless both defensible and valid.

So many cheeses are themselves nuanced that comparably nuanced wines are necessary. This is why, increasingly, the most serious lovers of cheese choose white wines over reds. This would have astounded our wine- and cheese-loving forebears.

Because of their greater delicacy, higher apparent acidity and flavor transparency (no intrusive tannins, for example) many modern white wines are better suited to many of today's best cheeses than today's red wines. The reason, of course, is comparable nuance.

You can try this for yourself, and very likely you will see why this modern preference among some cheese (and wine) lovers for serving white wines with cheeses is not just fashion, but informed fashion. With few exceptions, today's white wines are superior to anything made, say, 50 or 100 years ago. This is thanks to superior winemaking, better equipment and greater control, not only technologically, but also thanks to scientific educations that allow winemakers to be more astute in handling intrinsically more delicate white wines.

For cheeses, this collective renaissance of white wines has been a godsend. Try, for example, any of a number of what are called "grower Champagnes", which are small producer French Champagnes that typically offer more characterful, even idiosyncratic,

Champagnes than the mass-market *grandes marques* found in grocery stores and wine shops everywhere could possibly (or would dare) offer. Sample such a grower Champagne with, say, Parmigiano-Reggiano. Or with any number of other harder, dry cheeses.

Of course, red wine is hardly out of the picture. But if you focus on cheese, you will see nuance in wine more readily. More than most foods, cheese helps make one that much more aware of the necessity of nuance when faced with choosing which wine goes well with which foods.

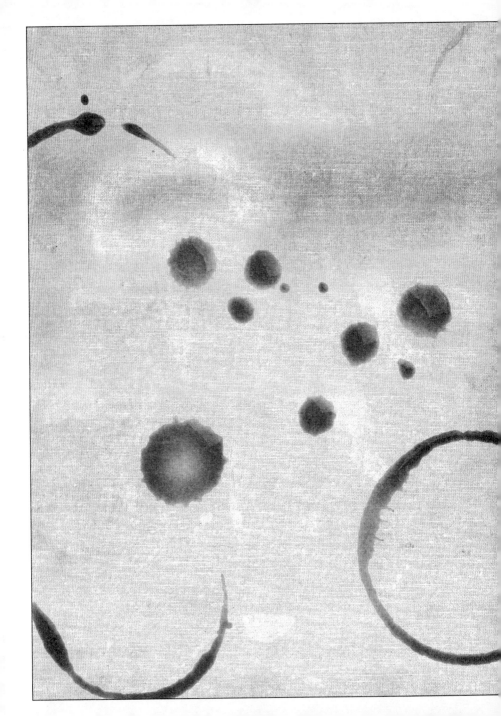

ENDNOTES

1. Despite its attractive simplicity, the sentence "Language shapes thought" must necessarily be acknowledged as an over-simplification. A vast number of research papers in cognitive psychology explore what's called "linguistic relativity." Opinions have seesawed over the past century, with much of the most recent research suggesting that while language can and does shape thought, it's neither absolute nor invariably deterministic.

That noted, there's little dispute any more about whether language can shape thought. "The past decade has seen a host of ingenious demonstrations establishing that language indeed plays a causal role in shaping cognition," says Lera Boroditsky, a university professor of cognitive science and author of numerous papers on the subject of language and thought. "Studies have shown that changing how people talk changes how they think. Teaching people new color words, for instance, changes their ability to discriminate colors. And teaching people a new way of talking about time gives them a new way of thinking about it." ("How Language Shapes Thought," *Scientific American*, February 2011)

2. Creating machines that can reliably and unerringly substitute human tasters has been the Holy Grail of sensory scientists for decades. Various food processing agencies involved with tea, coffee, wine and other

products strongly dependent upon human tasters have developed what are popularly known as "electronic tongues." All involve the use of electronic sensors that identify electrical conductivity or analyze the gases of particular ingredients.

A recent example is the creation of a gizmo in Thailand to establish and verify the "authenticity" of Thai dishes offered in restaurants. An article in *The New York Times* (September 28, 2014) reports that the wonderfully-named Thai Delicious Committee funded the development of a machine that "evaluates food by measuring its conductivity at different voltages. Readings from 10 sensors are combined to produce the chemical signature."

After evaluating the "authentic" electrical conductivity of the ingredients, the gizmo also gives a score on a 100-point scale: "A sample was placed in the stainless-steel tray, the machine made a whirring sound, and moments later it issued a score of 78 out of 100."

There's little doubt that these electronic sensory devices will grow ever more adept and sophisticated at identifying specific compounds or ingredients in various liquids and foods. What is less likely to develop to anything rivaling human capacity is an electronic ability to correlate the quantified data in such a way as to establish the "sum greater than its parts" harmony that creates our most gratifying sensory experiences.

3. Remember all that business about statistical validity mentioned previously? Here's what happened next with the peanut butter cookie and the 24 "correct answers" from the 60 tasters in the triangle test:

" $H0$: A=B Ha: A and B are not the same

A=reformulated product

B=original product

O_c=observed number of correct responses=24

E_c=n(1/3)=(60)(1/3)=20

O_I=observed number of incorrect responses=60-24=36

E_I=n(2/3)=(60)(2/3)=40

α=risk of a Type I error=0.05

From a chi-square distribution chart, $X^2 1, 0.05$=3.84

Since $X2$=0.48<3.84, we fail to reject the null hypothesis and conclude that there is no significant difference between samples A and B. In other words, the reformulated cookie is not significantly different from the original cookie."

4. Rudolf Arnheim, *Art and Visual Perception: A Psychology of the Creative Eye*, New Version, 1974.

5. A recent example of this is physicist Richard Taylor's exploration of the fractal nature of Jackson Pollock's ostensibly inchoate drip or splatter paintings. Mathematicians rank fractal dimensions on a scale of 0 to

3. Most natural objects, when analyzed in two dimensions, rank between 1.2 and 1.6.

An article in *Discover* magazine (November 2001) reports: "Taylor collaborated with perceptual psychologists in Australia and England… The team began by dividing fractal patterns into three categories: natural, computer-generated, and man-made—the last category consisting of cropped sections of Pollock's drip paintings. They then asked 50 subjects to evaluate about 40 different patterns each, with each subject having to choose between two patterns at a time. The results, published in *Nature* last March, were conclusive: Subjects preferred fractal dimensions between 1.3 and 1.5, regardless of their origin, roughly 80 percent of the time.

"The same predisposition seems to be at work in other mediums as well. Studies have found that people prefer patterns that are neither too regular, like the test bars on a television channel, nor too random, like a snowy screen. They prefer the subtle variations on a recurring theme in, say, a Beethoven concerto, to the monotony of repeated scales or the cacophony of someone pounding on a keyboard."

6. In fact, Amerine and his coauthor, Professor Edward B. Roessler, put forth a list of 113 words that met with their disapproval. The list was prefaced with this disclaimer: "It is not our intent to condemn the

"All the experience in the world is of little use unless its primary objective is acquiring and transmitting insight. The only question a reader need ask when evaluating a wine writer is: How much insight is he or she seeking to provide?"

following terms (although some of them deserve it) for your wine vocabulary, but merely to warn you to use them with caution, if at all."

Like an unusually severe (itself an unacceptable wine term) monastic order, aspiring wine monks were urged to renounce terms such as *austere, chewy, coarse, delicate, elegant, fat, finesse, flabby, flinty, full, hard, harsh, intense, metallic, powerful, pungent, rich, robust, silky, smoky, supple, tough* and *velvety*, among others.

7. L.B. Meyer: 'Meaning in Music and Information Theory', *Journal of Aesthetics and Art Criticism*, xv (1957), 412–24

8. Matthew M. Lavy: "The Creative Audience: Listening As Narrative Process", University of Cambridge (no date given)

9. In the 1990s, Linda Bartoshuk, a professor at the Yale University School of Medicine made a big splash with research that showed that people can be divided into three groups: nontasters, regular tasters and supertasters.

Supertasters, she says, have more taste buds than others—as much as 100 times as many taste buds per square centimeter compared to a nontaster. It is strictly an inherited trait. Roughly one-quarter of the population are so endowed. Another one-quarter are nontasters and the remaining half of the population are regular sorts.

Bartoshuk reports that women generally have more taste buds than men. Then comes the clincher: Two-thirds of all the supertasters are women.

Being a supertaster would seem an incontestable boon. The problem with having a lot of taste buds is that taste sensations are intensified to the point of pain. Supertasters, Professor Bartoshuk reports, typically dislike spicy foods, which irritate, as do fatty foods, which literally weigh upon the touch sensors in the fungiform papillae. (Supertasters also have more sensitive touch receptors in their tongues.)

Being a so-called supertaster is as much a prescription for painful sensitivity as it is an asset. A supertaster has to work around her genetic inheritance as much as with it.

10. Let me give you an example. While researching this chapter I went online to consult the Merriam-Webster dictionary Web site for the definition of nuance: "1: a subtle distinction or variation; 2: a subtle quality: nicety; 3: sensibility to, awareness of, or ability to express delicate shadings (as of meaning, feeling, or value)."

Here's the kicker. Merriam-Webster asks users of their Web site "What made you want to look up nuance?

Please tell us where you read or heard it."

A guy from Houston named Rob (whose full name was cited, but who shall go unidentified here) answered: "To me, it is a flakey, funky, and femmie sounding word I hear too much."

I ask you: What kind of wines is our guy Rob likely to prefer?

11. "In terms of pure alcohol, consumption of beer has more than halved since the peak in the mid-1970s, and is now at the lowest level since 1945-46.... Beer still comprised the greatest proportion of all pure alcohol consumed in Australia at 41%, followed by wine (37%)..." (Source: Australian Bureau of Statistics Bulletin 4307.0.55.001: "Apparent Consumption of Alcohol, Australia, 2012-13")

12. "Americans who drink alcohol are about equally likely to say they drink beer (36%) or wine (35%) most often. ... That continues the trend in which beer has declined as the preferred beverage of U.S. drinkers, shrinking its advantage over wine from 20 percentage points in 1992 to one point today." (Source: Gallup Poll, August 1, 2013: "U.S. Drinkers Divide Between Beer and Wine as Favorite"

ABOUT THE AUTHOR

Matt Kramer has been a full-time independent wine writer since 1976. His column appears in every issue of *Wine Spectator*, in addition to a twice-monthly Web column on WineSpectator.com. He has previously also been the wine critic for the *Los Angeles Times*, *The Oregonian* and *The New York Sun* newspapers.

Matt Kramer is the author of eight critically acclaimed books: *Making Sense of Wine; Making Sense of Burgundy; Making Sense of California Wine; A Passion For Piedmont: Italy's Most Glorious Regional Table; Making Sense of Wine—Second Edition; Matt Kramer's New California Wine; Matt Kramer's Making Sense of Italian Wine* and *Matt Kramer On Wine*, a collection of his best columns and essays over the years. His books have been translated into Korean, Japanese and Swedish.

He divides his time between Portland, Oregon and San Francisco.

ABOUT CIDER MILL PRESS BOOK PUBLISHERS

Good ideas ripen with time. From seed to harvest, Cider Mill Press brings fine reading, information, and entertainment together between the covers of its creatively crafted books. Our Cider Mill bears fruit twice a year, publishing a new crop of titles each spring and fall.

VISIT US ON THE WEB AT
www.cidermillpress.com

OR WRITE TO US AT
12 Spring Street
PO Box 454
Kennebunkport, Maine 04046

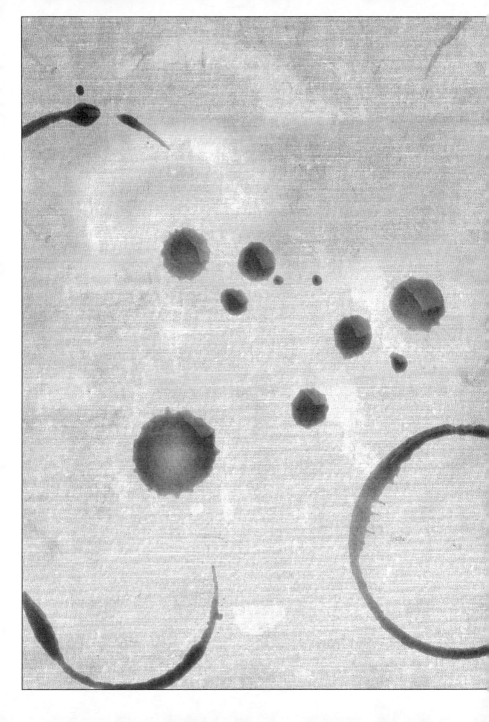